Beyond Reasonable Doubt

The Billie-Jo Jenkins Case Revisited

by Dr David Holding

First published by
Words Are Life, 2023
www.wordsarelife.co.uk

First published in Great Britain in 2023 by
Words are Life
10 Chester Place,
Adlington, Chorley, PR6 9RP
wordsarelife@mail.com
www.wordsarelife.co.uk

Electronic version and paperback versions available for purchase on Amazon.
Copyright (c) Dr David Holding and Words are Life.

First edition 2023.

Acknowledgements

I am most grateful for the support I have received from many sources in both my research and preparation for this work. In particular, I wish to thank members of both the medical and legal professions for the generosity and benefit of their expertise and opinions on the issues presented by this specific case. My sincere thanks must also go to those ever-obliging staff at the law libraries and archives I have consulted. My gratitude loses no sincerity in its generality.

The primary source for this work has been the comprehensive account of the case in Sion Jenkins' and Bob Woffinden's publication, *The Murder of Billie-Jo* that was produced in 2008. This has been supplemented by the full official transcripts of the Appeals of 1999 and 2004, which have been consulted and analysed. A selection of articles and media reports have also been valuable reference material. These provide the reader with a varied but comprehensive overview of this tragic yet highly-publicised case.

Finally, but never least, my sincere gratitude goes to my publisher, Lesley Atherton. Her total commitment and support for my work never diminishes.

Dr David Holding, 2023

About the Author

Dr David Holding studied history at Manchester University before entering the teaching profession in the 1970s. He taught in both state and independent sectors. During this time, he continued historical research culminating in both a Master's degree and a Doctorate. Having previously studied law, David gained a Master of Law degree in Medical Law, which enabled him to transfer to teaching legal courses at university. Since retiring, David has concentrated his research and writing on various aspects of local history, legal trials, forensic science and medico-legal topics.

Also by David Holding

Murder in the Heather: The Winter Hill Murder of 1838
This book is a unique account of a brutal murder that occurred on the summit of Winter Hill in Lancashire in 1838. The account draws on both contemporary media reports and court transcripts and examines the events leading to the killing of a 21-year-old packman. It details the trial proceedings of the only suspect in the case. The work concludes with a re-assessment of the case in the light of modern forensic investigation. The reader is invited to reach their own 'verdict' based on the evidence provided.

The Pendle Witch Trials of 1612
The book provides readers with a sequential overview of the famous chain of events that ultimately led to the execution of women accused of practising witchcraft in the county of Lancashire. It is presented as a chronological account of the famous trials at Lancaster Castle in 1612. This book introduces the evidence and interview transcripts that formed the major plank of the prosecution case and will appeal to both the general reader and local historian.

The Dark Figure: Crime in Victorian Bolton
This book provides an absorbing overview of crime in the Lancashire town of Bolton over the period 1850 to 1890. It is primarily based on documentary survey and analysis of court and police records covering the period. It assesses changes in crime over time and asks whether these relate to economic, social or political changes taking place at the same time. The reader is left to reflect on whether crime (in all its many forms) has changed over time.

Bleak Christmas: The Pretoria Colliery Disaster of 1910
This work charts the events of the Lancashire Pretoria Pit disaster in December 1910. It reflects on the devastation it left to many local communities whose main source of employment was coal. The main sources analysed are the Home Office Report on the disaster and the Report of the Inquest. The findings of these detailed legal reports are presented in a format that will supplement existing material on the event. The book will also provide a reference source for both local historians and the interested general reader.

Doctors in the Dock: The Trials of Doctors Harold Shipman, John Bodkin Adams and Buck Ruxton
This book takes the reader on a journey into the world of three medical doctors in England, each coming from a different social background but with one common thread going through their lives. They all stood trial for murder. In each case, the reader is presented with all relevant evidence available to jurors in the case. The overall aim of this work is to invite readers to exercise their judgment in reaching a verdict.

Forensic Science Basics: Every Contact Leaves a Trace
This work is an absorbing introductory study of the techniques familiar from numerous trials, media reports and TV crime dramas. It begins with the basic principles of forensic science then examines such aspects as the time of death, causes of death, weapons of crime, identification of offenders and much more. It provides essential reading for those who wish to gain a basic introduction to this fascinating area of science.

A Warning from History: The Influenza Pandemic of 1918
The 1918 Influenza Pandemic was one of the deadliest events in human history, and understanding the events and experience of 1918 is of great importance to pandemic preparation. This book aims to address questions concerning the pandemic's origin, features and causes to provide the reader with an appreciation of the 1918 pandemic and its

implications for future pandemics. This work caters to both the science-orientated and general reader in this crucial area of global and public health.

The Lady Chatterley Trial Revisited

The 1960 obscenity trial of Lady Chatterley's Lover remains a symbol of freedom of expression. It is also a seminal case in British literary and social history and credited as the catalyst which encouraged frank discussion of sexual behaviour. This book introduces readers to the trial itself, describing the prosecution and defence opening and closing speeches to the jury, and much more before culminating in the judge's summing-up and the final verdict. The reader is provided with all the evidence to reach a considered assessment of the case and a question to consider – can certain literature actually corrupt, or does it simply encourage expensive court trials and boost sales?

The Oscar Wilde Trials Revisited

It is only given to very few people to be the principal figure in three Old Bailey trials, before three different judges, and at three consecutive court sessions, all in one year. This complexity is one of the fascinations of the 1895 Oscar Wilde trials. In addition, they embodied celebrity, sex, humorous dialogue, outstanding displays of advocacy, political intrigue woven with issues of art and morality. Wilde's prosecution of the Marquess of Queensberry from criminal libel, and Wilde's later prosecution for 'gross indecency', reveal a complex person at odds with a class-centred and morally ambiguous Victorian society. This work considers these famous trials in chronological sequence and invites the reader to participate as an observer and potential juror in the proceedings. Finally, the reader is encouraged to consider the evidence presented at each trial and arrive at their own conclusions. This work will be of particular interest to law students owing to the counsel's skilfully demonstrated advocacy skills. It also caters for the general reader with a particular interest in the presentation of criminal cases in the courts in England.

The Whitechapel Murders of 1888

The killing of five women in the Whitechapel area of East London in 1888 remains the greatest and most horrendous of all unsolved murder mysteries. It is the classic cold case. This work takes a novel look into the case from the perspective of the criminal investigation itself. In this approach, the more speculative and conspiracy theories surrounding the Jack the Ripper crimes have been avoided. The reader is offered insights into these murders by employing the modern forensic techniques of geographical and offender profiling, which shed new light on these serial killings.

Forensic Pathology Basics: The Dead Do Tell a Story
In this work, the reader is taken on a sequential journey of discovery into the fascinating world of Forensic Pathology, with no previous knowledge of the subject being required of readers. Beginning with the initial discovery of a body, the reader experiences the processes involving the forensic pathologist, from the initial examination and identification of the deceased to the final autopsy. The reader will be introduced to practical applications of the pathologist's skills and techniques at each stage. Past criminal cases will be introduced to demonstrate the variety of scenarios in which the assistance of the forensic pathologist is vital. The overall aim of this work is to provide the reader with a fascinating insight into the largely unseen involvement of the forensic pathologist in death investigations. It is especially fascinating when the circumstances involve criminal activity. The manner and causes of death are discussed in detail and cover the main areas of injury. A glossary of medical terminology is provided to explain the various terms used in the text. The work concludes with a selected bibliography to enable the reader to pursue their research in those areas they find particularly interesting and relevant.

The Coronavirus Pandemic: An English Perspective
The Coronavirus (COVID-19) pandemic of 2020 onwards has been described as the second most deadly event in recent human history. The first was attributed to the influenza pandemic of 1918. A comparison has been made between the two events because of the similarities regarding high mortality and because of the resultant impact the pandemics had on the social and economic structures of the countries involved. This work provides the reader with a comprehensive background to the virus's origins, its subsequent rapid spread in England, and the government's responses and control policies implemented to halt its progress. This work will be of interest to both the science-orientated and the general reader with concern in this vital area of public health and in the preparation for future pandemics.

Live Or Let Die? The Euthanasia Debate Revisited
Euthanasia is concerned with decisions relating to the end of life, and is a major focus for public, academic and legal debate. Emotional responses dominate and range from calls for more liberalisation to dire warnings that society has now embarked upon a slippery slope. The

legal and ethical issues which flow from the euthanasia debate encompass a wide range of matters which permeate medical law by questioning the respective roles of both the medical and legal professions. This work considers definitions of euthanasia, case studies and related law in the UK and Netherlands. This work emphasises the powerful struggle that exists in law, medicine and ethics regarding the nature, scope and foundations of the right to choose the manner of one's own death. Our thought-provoking conclusion considers: "Under what conditions, if any, is it permissible for patients and health professionals to intentionally end life?"

The Psychological Aspects of Eyewitness Evidence
Eyewitness evidence is typically given the most credibility in courts of law. However, it should be admitted with caution and a clear understanding that certain psychological factors can its reliability. This work invites the reader to consider these factors. Each chapter in the work considers the various stages involved in eyewitness testimony in courts of law, from the initial witnessing of an event, the questioning stage and culminating in the court trial itself, and the evidence's presentation. This work poses two questions for the reader to consider: "Exactly how reliable is eyewitness testimony?" and "What factors impact the accuracy of such evidence?"

Forensic Science Basics: Every Contact Leaves a Trace
This book covers such topics as time of death, causes of death, weapons used in crime, identity of offenders, bloodstain analysis and document examination. By following this chronological sequence, the reader becomes an active participant in the whole process of investigating crime. Each chapter covers a specific area of forensic interest and begins with an informative description of the various investigative techniques involved in the analysis of specific forms of evidence. It is impossible to cover all of forensic science at an introductory level, so the aim of this work is to provide readers with the opportunity to appreciate the basic principles behind criminal investigation. The work concludes with a selected bibliography to enable interested readers to pursue their own research into this fascinating area of science.

Justice Delayed: Hillsborough Revisited
This work will provide readers with a detailed synopsis of the official inquiries launched in the aftermath of the Hillsborough disaster, together with a review of the new inquests and the criminal trials which followed. The work also constitutes an account of how the British

establishment failed at every level to deliver justice. It records a catalogue of failings in response to a major disaster. In many respects, this work contains all the elements of a grand scale conspiracy which went right to the top of the establishment. This persisted because of collusion between the elites in politics, the police, and the media. It also reveals how the Hillsborough families prevailed against all the odds, and retained their dignity in the face of great adversity. The reader is left to consider one vital question in relation to this tragedy: "How did parliament allow such injustice on this scale to remain for so long? It was the enduring conspiracy of lies and deceit that stands as the most damning indictment of how the Hillsborough disaster was handled. The lasting lesson from this disaster is that there must never again, be any arbitrary time limit on justice and accountability.

INTRODUCTION

Billie-Jo Margaret Jenkins was a 13-year-old girl who was brutally murdered on 15 February 1997 in Hastings, East Sussex. She was originally brought up in East London, with her father imprisoned and her mother unable to cope on her own.

Billie-Jo was placed in foster care from the age of nine with Sion and Lois Jenkins, who coincidentally had the same surname but were not related. The couple already had four daughters of their own.

Billie-Jo's foster-father, Sion Jenkins, had started teaching in a number of schools within the London area. In 1992, he applied for the post of deputy headteacher at the William Parker School in Hastings, East Sussex. On securing this position, the Jenkins family moved from London to Hastings in August 1992.

Billie-Jo moved with the family and attended Helenswood School in Hastings. She had been living with the Jenkins family for five years prior to her death in February 1997. She was described as being a 'fun-loving' child who wanted to become an actor.

At the time of the murder, this case gained widespread media attention and to date, the case remains unsolved. Within the space of one month following the death, Billie-Jo's foster-father, deputy headteacher Sion Jenkins, became the prime suspect.

He was arrested, charged and convicted of the crime at a trial held in 1998. However, following two appeals and two further re-trials, Jenkins was formally acquitted of the crime in February 2006. In both of these re-trials in 2005, the juries were unable to reach a verdict.

Jenkins spent six years in prison following his

conviction, but, on his acquittal, he was denied compensation for the time spent in prison. This was on the grounds that there was no evidence to prove his innocence of the crime. This was, apparently essential in order to be considered for compensation payments.

He had been declared 'Not Guilty' at the second re-trial by the judge. It appears that Sion Jenkins holds the rare distinction of having been acquitted of murder, but has never been found 'Not Guilty' by a jury. A second charge of 'obtaining a pecuniary advantage by deception' in that he lied about his academic qualifications to obtain the post in Hastings, was not pursued, but 'left to lie on file'.

Sussex Police have maintained that there are no plans to re-open the investigation into Billie-Jo's murder. However, in January 2022, they did announce that as part of a regular 'cold-case review', they would be re-examining the available evidence from the crime scene to see if advances in forensic science since 1997 could lead to a breakthrough in the case. They also assured the public that any new information received which may lead to new lines of enquiry, will always be considered.

Billie-Jo's natural family have always maintained that Sion Jenkins was guilty of Billie-Jo's murder, and have blamed the outcome of the final re-trial on the judge's ruling that new forensic evidence obtained by the prosecution was deemed inadmissible. This was due to a procedural oversight on the part of the prosecution, having failed to disclose this new evidence in time for the defence to examine and respond to it. The judge considered this to be disadvantageous to the defence.

The aim of this work is to consider and analyse the evidence presented by both the prosecution and defence over the course of three criminal trials and two appeals. In so doing, it may be possible to answer two critical questions which this case raises.

Did the police have the right suspect in the first place,

or was an innocent man wrongly convicted of a crime that he did not, or could not, have committed?

Analysis of the case reveals that Sion Jenkins became the target of a lynch-mob mentality in the public's eye. This was certainly fuelled to a large extent by media frenzy which was also reinforced by the seemingly endless legal processes Sion Jenkins had to endure.

This work also exposes failings in the criminal justice system in terms of its administration. There was what some observers of the case have described as deliberate "tainting" of the Jenkins's children's statements to the police following the murder, together with a concerted effort to influence the statements made by Lois, Jenkin's former wife.

To assist the reader, the work follows a chronological format of events, beginning with the relevant backgrounds of the main families involved in the tragedy. This is followed by an examination of the police investigation itself and the interviewing of witnesses. Included are details of two other suspects of interest to the inquiry, both of whom were eventually eliminated from the investigation.

A chapter is devoted to a detailed analysis of the forensic evidence presented by both prosecution and defence, because this formed the main strand in the prosecution and defence of Sion Jenkins. A chapter is devoted to media response to the crime. The work concludes with a retrospective overview of the case.

Taken as a whole, the work will provide the reader with the opportunity to consider a case which has become one of the greatest *causes celebre* in British criminal history. Here the reader is invited to consider the evidence presented to the juries in the three criminal trials. With the benefit of this information, it is hoped that the reader will be in a position to reach their own considered verdict in this thought-provoking criminal case. It is also hoped that the work will contribute to, and possibly encourage, a quest to expose those who bear the responsibility for this horrific and senseless crime.

CHAPTER ONE

EARLY BEGINNINGS

Sion David Charles Jenkins was born on 12 July 1957 in Greenwich, South London. His parents were David and Megan Jenkins, and David was a former police officer (he had been with the Metropolitan Police for five years).

In 1962, David joined the Michelin tyre company which entailed a lot of travelling. As a result, the family moved to Scotland (Brookfield on the outskirts of Glasgow).

Sion attended Glasgow Academy as a teenager. When his father was offered promotion within the Michelin company, the family moved back to London. Whilst in London, Sion attended Windsor and Eton College of Further Education to complete his A level studies. On completion, he accepted an offer on a course of study in Physical Education and English at Nonington College of Physical Education in Canterbury. After obtaining his Teachers' Certificate in Education, he obtained a post as supply teaching at Stepney Green boys' school in London.

He met Lois Bale, a nurse at the Royal London Hospital in Whitechapel, and they married on the 18 December, 1982. They had four daughters; Annie Victoria, born 12 June, 1984; Charlotte Mary, born 19 March, 1986; Esther Louise, born 12 February, 1988 and Maya Cornelia, born 4 November, 1989.

In 1989, Sion was appointed head of faculty of communications at McKentee School in Walthamstow. The department included English, foreign languages, careers and IT. It was during this period that Sion studied for an

MSc degree in education management at the University of East London, gaining his degree in November, 1992. He applied for the post of deputy headteacher at the William Parker boys' comprehensive school in Hastings, East Sussex. On securing the post, Sion and the family moved to Hastings in August 1992.

Billie-Jo Margaret Jenkins was born on 29 March 1983 to Deborah (Debbie) Barrett and Bayard (Bill) Jenkins in the East End of London. Debbie and Bill first met whilst Bill was in Wandsworth Prison serving time for assaulting a police officer. A friend of Debbie's had a partner in the prison and asked Debbie to accompany her on a prison visit to see her partner and another friend who turned out to be Bill Jenkins. Debbie and Bill began a relationship, and when he was released, he moved in with Debbie. The couple married six weeks after the birth of Billie-Jo in 1983.

Billie-Jo's mother Debbie had a drink problem and had been arrested for credit card fraud. She struggled to care for and house her children. When Bill Jenkins was sent back to prison, Billie-Jo and her siblings were sent to live with other family members. Billie-Jo was eight years old at the time. After short periods with a grandmother and an aunt, she and her brother were placed in foster care, first in Ilford, Essex. This placement did not last long.

Lois Jenkins answered a social services advertisement for foster parents in her local newspaper. At this time, Lois was a social worker, and her husband a teacher. They lived in Bow, East London at the time with their four natural daughters. Both Billie-Jo and her brother were initially placed with the Jenkins family. However, at some point, the boy moved back to his birth family, but nine-year-old Billie-Jo stayed on a long-term basis with the Jenkins. The two sets of Jenkins were not related to each other, the shared name was completely coincidental.

A few weeks after Billie-Jo's arrival with the Jenkins

family, Sion Jenkins was appointed deputy headteacher in Hastings. It does appear that Billie-Jo was enthusiastic about being part of the Jenkins family and made the move to Hastings with them.

For most part, Billie-Jo was seen as a happy, stable and well-adjusted teenager. The house which to Jenkins family moved to was a large, three-storey, semi-detached property in Lower Park Road, Hastings overlooking Alexandra Park. The street itself could be described as 'comfortably middle class'. However, Hastings did have some problems with criminal activity, so it was not so clear-cut to divide the town into good and bad areas.

In 1996, over one thousand local residents in Hastings signed a petition for better security for Alexandra Park. This was a place frequented by drug users and underage drinkers. In the same year, two girls were sexually assaulted and two people were murdered elsewhere in Hastings. Several neighbours of the Jenkins reported that there has been a spate of robberies as well as vandalism in the area.

CHAPTER TWO

THE FATEFUL DAY

On the afternoon of Saturday 15 February, 1997, Lois Jenkins had taken her two youngest daughters, Esther and Maya, for a walk along the local beach in Hastings. Lotte was at a clarinet lesson with a school friend. It had been agreed that Sion would collect Lotte after her lesson finished.

In the meantime, Sion, Annie and Billie-Jo were at home. Both of the girls were earning pocket money by doing jobs in the house and garden. Billie-Jo was keen to earn some money for a pair of trainers she had seen in the town and Sion had agreed she could buy them.

Annie's job was to clear out a utility room at the rear of the house. She found a set of large tent pegs, together with other items. She placed these pegs on top of the coal bunker in the rear garden.

Billie-Jo had already started to paint the patio doors leading into the rear garden. Annie understood that she would either be taking over from, or assisting Billie-Jo with the painting later in the day.

On finishing the clearing out of the utility room, Annie's next job was to wash the family's Opel car which was parked outside the front of the house on the main road. The Jenkins family owned three cars, a Citroen being used mainly by Lois, the Opel and a white MG convertible sports car, mainly used by Sion.

In the afternoon of Saturday 15 February, Sion asked Annie if she wanted to go with him to collect Lottie and her friend from the clarinet lesson, and she agreed. At around

3:00 pm, they left in the MG, while Billie-Jo stayed at home to continue with the painting. Sion and Annie collected both Lotte and her friend from the clarinet lesson, dropped her friend off at her home, and came back home. Lotte then dropped off her clarinet in her bedroom.

It was at this point that Sion told Annie and Lotte that they needed to go to a local DIY store and buy some white spirit. This was for Annie to assist Billie-Jo with the painting, and because Billie-Jo had spilt some paint on the patio tiles. It would appear that Sion must have seen Billie-Jo when they returned and noticed the spilt paint, hence the reason for the sudden visit to the DIY store.

Sion could not have been alone on the patio for more than three minutes at most. The most direct route to the store was to head left from the Jenkins' home. However, on this occasion Sion headed right instead, which involved taking a circuitous route taking him around the local Alexandra Park. The reason for this was that his MG sports car was parked facing to the right. It was easier for him to just drive in that direction rather than having to do a three-point turn to go the other way.

There was only about 0.3 miles/0.5 km difference between the two routes. However, the rest of this journey appears rather odd. Before turning off for the DIY store, Sion suddenly decided that by this time, it was too late for Annie to start painting and headed back home. This occurrence makes little sense, since Sion stated that he needed the white spirit for spillages, irrespective of whether Annie was going to paint or otherwise. However, before he reached home, he changed his mind once again, and looped back to the DIY store. On arriving at the car park, he then discovered he did not have any money to pay for anything. So, he did not enter the store but instead drove directly back home.

On arrival back home, Lotte ran ahead of Sion and Annie into the house, and was the first to discover Billie-

Jo's body lying on the patio with blood around her head. She cries out to Sion who ushers both girls into a playroom in the house and then calls 999. This call was logged at 3:38 pm. Billie-Jo had been beaten to death in the back garden, with an 18-inch (45cm) tent-peg weighing 2lbs (0.9kg).

The murder weapon was found by her body on the ground. She was lying on the patio, her head on a black bin-liner, and she was fully clothed, with no signs of sexual assault. The house did not appear to have been burgled or any forced entry obvious. When asked by the emergency operator if his daughter was breathing, Sion stated that he didn't know because he hadn't looked. He estimated the timing of the incident at between half-and three-quarters of an hour earlier.

After making the first emergency call, Sion phoned his near neighbour, Denise Lancaster, informing her that there had been an accident. She arrived quickly and was directed to the dining room and out onto the patio at the rear of the house. Sion stated that he touched Billie-Jo's neck at some point and felt it to be warm. He described her eyes as swollen and her head as misshapen. He went inside the house to wash the blood off his hands.

Denise told Sion to call the emergency services again and stress the urgency of the situation. Sion makes this second emergency call which was logged at 3:46 pm.

Denise noticed that something had been stuffed into Billie-Jo's left nostril. When she pulled it out, she discovered that it was part of the black bin liner her head was lying on. A flow of blood was released from the girl's nose as Denise removed the liner.

When the ambulance eventually arrived, it was noted by the paramedics attending the scene that Sion did not come out onto the patio as they attended to Billie-Jo. Instead, he went out to the front of the property and just sat in his MG sports car. This was considered unusual.

Shortly after the ambulance, police officers arrived. They had responded to the ambulance call. The scene was then declared a crime scene and detectives began to arrive to begin an investigation.

CHAPTER THREE

MURDER INVESTIGATION

The criminal investigation was led by Detective Superintendent Jeremy Paine of Sussex Police, and it initially focussed on a mentally ill man who was seen in the area of the killing around the same time as the murder was committed. Reports began emerging of a man with obvious mental difficulties wandering in the vicinity of the crime. He was easily recognisable because (according to one witness) he had a prominent scar on his face, which extended from his forehead down towards his left cheek.

The movements of this man on that day were easily established. In the morning he went into the main branch of the Nat West bank in Hastings, claiming to have lost some cheques. The bank assistant described him as "weird and rather threatening". He then went into Safeways about an hour after Lois Jenkins had been there with three of her children. He informed the check-out assistant that he had been poisoned by milk he had bought there. He then headed away from the town centre towards Alexandra Park.

One witness who was working on his car said the man gave the impression that he had some mental condition. Several other people felt disconcerted by the appearance of this man.

At about 3:00 pm on the Saturday afternoon, the man knocked on the door of 59, Lower Park Road, which was a well-established guest house. The proprietor Brian Kent, stated that the man asked about accommodation, but he wouldn't have considered offering him any. He described the man as obviously suffering from mental health issues.

Mr Kent advised him to go back towards Hastings town centre. He did go down the road but turned in the general direction of number 48, Lower Park Road, the Jenkins' house.

In the middle of the Saturday afternoon, there were numerous sightings of this man in Alexandra Park. One witness saw him as she was going down to the cafe in the park with her young son. This was about 3:00 pm. On her way back from the cafe, she saw him again between 3:55 and 4:00 pm. Another witness stated that his attention had been drawn to the man because "he had his finger poked up his nose".

Since the majority of these witnesses noticed a prominent facial scar, locals began to question whether these sightings were connected to an assault on a 12-year-old girl a few months earlier. This man was identified almost instantly by the police because two of the witnesses knew him personally. The first of these witnesses, a psychiatric nurse, saw him at about 2:30 pm. The second, a nursing assistant who was out walking with her boyfriend, saw him coming towards them in the street at about 4:00 pm. She had been employed at a local hospital and immediately recognised him.

This man was identified as Mark Lynam who was in his 40s and had a long history of mental illness. It appears that on the previous day, an attempt had been made to section him under the Mental Health Act. A response team had visited his flat but he was not at home. Apparently, the team appeared to have abandoned their task until the weekend. He was last seen on the Saturday at around 5:30 pm walking along the sea front at Hastings in the direction of nearby St Leonards (where he lived).

Mark Lynam was back at home on the Sunday when the police called at lunchtime to arrest him on suspicion of the murder of Billie-Jo Jenkins. A local resident produced a spare key to Lynam's flat provided by Lynam's father.

Lynam was in the flat and rushed out of the front door, knocking one of the officers WDC Briggs to the ground. This officer attempted to restrain him but was kicked.

With the help of a member of the public, and two other officers who had responded to the call for assistance, together with a member of the public, Mark Lynam was finally restrained.

He was taken to Hastings police station where according to the custody Sergeant, he "remained very violent and uncooperative". During the police search of Mark Lynam, three pieces of blue plastic were discovered. He remained in police custody overnight to allow him to calm down. At approximately 3:48 pm on the Sunday afternoon, Lynam was informed that he had been arrested on suspicion of murder and was duly cautioned.

At 4:00 pm, Dr Joseph Ludwig, a police surgeon arrived and examined him. At 7.00 pm police searched Lynam's flat but nothing of significance was recovered. Whilst in police custody, a duty solicitor, consultant psychiatrist and a social worker had all arrived at Hastings police station. Each had a respective statutory duty to safeguard Lynam's welfare.

At approximately 9:30 pm on the Sunday, Brian Kent, the guest-house proprietor arrived at the police station in response to a request to make a "confirmation identification". He confirmed that Lynam was the man who had called at his premises at approximately 3:00 pm on the Saturday afternoon.

The consultant psychiatrist, Dr Weppner, reported:

"This man is well-known to our service, and suffers from chronic paranoid schizophrenia. There is no previous history of violence. He needs to be eliminated positively or negatively from the current enquiry. He has a set of grandiose delusions about his station in life. He is not fit to be interviewed for the inquiry. We also feel that he is not fit to be released on bail and is a potential danger to the

public".

The following day, Monday 17 February, Mr Lynam spent the day again in police custody and then at approximately 11:00 pm on the Tuesday, he was once again examined and then at 12:55 am on the Wednesday, he was released from Hastings police station and detained under the Mental Health Act. He was released into the care of Eastbourne NHS Trust, was taken to a secure psychiatric unit and detained there.

Following the detention of Mark Lynam, police attention had shifted, and on Wednesday 19 February, they arrested a second suspect, a local Hastings resident, Felix Simmons. Sion Jenkin's wife, Lois, and a friend, Peter Gaimster, considered him to be a likely suspect and had pointed the police in his direction. It transpired that Simmons had suffered a mental breakdown the previous summer which had resulted in police being called out a number of times, due to what Lois had described as "Felix's violent behaviour".

As part of the initial house-to-house inquiries following the murder of Billie-Jo, Simmons and Suzanne (his wife who was a solicitor) were interviewed separately. Within hours of the murder Suzanne answered preliminary inquiries by stating that she and her husband had been talking in the kitchen during the afternoon of Saturday 15 February. On Sunday, Simmons himself stated that he had been at home all day until about 8:30 pm when he and his wife went out.

One reason for Simmons' arrest was that officers noticed that he had splashes of white paint on his clothing, whereas he was actually painting the kitchen yellow. On Wednesday 19 February, officers again went to Simmons' home and his wife told them that he was out at work. They requested that on his return he reported to Hastings police station.

Simmons arrived alone at 9:00 pm and was then

arrested on suspicion of the murder of Billie-Jo. His clothing was sent to the forensic laboratory. Senior officers decided that he could not be interviewed until both a psychiatric nurse and the duty solicitor could be present. It was twenty minutes past midnight when officers finally began interviewing Simmons.

He gave an account of his movements for the day of the murder. He reiterated that he had only been out of the house for about 45 minutes at around lunchtime. At about 8:30 pm he and Suzanne went out for the evening after his in-laws arrived to baby-sit. They returned soon after 10:00 pm and then he walked his in-laws back to their car. As he walked back to his house, a neighbour told him that Billie-Jo had "fallen through some glass" and had been killed.

Having provided his account, Simmons was taken back to his police cell for the night. The following day was Thursday 20 February and Suzanne Simmons spent much of the morning phoning the police station. She complained about the fact that they'd held her husband in a cell overnight, and also emphasised that she did not want him represented by the duty solicitor.

Suzanne had arranged for a different solicitor to attend. The second interview took place that same afternoon. This time things were very different. The new solicitor told police that his client had already provided a full account of his movements on the day of the murder and he advised Simmons to give 'No Comment' responses to further questions.

Meanwhile, other officers took a statement from Suzanne Simmons. This made it clear that she could provide a firm alibi for her husband, as he was with her throughout the afternoon of Saturday 15 February 1997. It had also by now been established that the 'white splashes' the officers thought they had discovered on Simmons' clothing were in fact, yellow, the colour he was using to decorate his kitchen.

That same evening, a taxi-driver who had spotted someone walking briskly down the path away from 48, Lower Park Road (the Jenkins' house) arrived at Hastings police station. At 6:47 pm Simmons was put on an identity parade. The taxi-driver did not pick him out.

Simmons' fingerprints were taken, together with DNA samples. He was then released without charge from police custody at 8:25 pm. He had been held for just 35 minutes short of the 24-hour maximum.

INTERVIEWS WITH ANNIE AND CHARLOTTE JENKINS

On Sunday 16 February 1997, police conducted video interviews with Jenkins' two eldest daughters Annie (12) and Charlotte (10). Both children had been with their father, Sion, throughout the previous afternoon, the day of the murder.

These interviews centred on what had occurred between 3:00 and 4:00pm on Saturday 15 February. In particular, this would include the journey to collect Charlotte from her clarinet lesson and return home, and the aborted journey to the DIY store and the second return home, concluding with the discovery of fatally injured Billie-Jo.

Charlotte was the first to be interviewed beginning at 3:50 pm. The interviewer explained that he required Charlotte to describe what happened on the Saturday afternoon. She began by saying that they went to the DIY store, but Sion had forgotten his money so they returned home. She mentioned that before they took the journey to the DIY store, she noticed that the garden gate was shut and when they returned it was open.

She told how she ran upstairs to drop off her clarinet in her bedroom. When she came back downstairs, she noticed the gate was shut again. She then recounted that when they realised that they had forgotten the money, her father said it was too far to go back home and then return to the store, so they went straight back home. When they arrived back home, they all got out of the car and went back into the house. Charlotte again mentioned that she noticed that the gate was once again open. In particular, she could see the rabbit hutch beyond the gate.

Charlotte went into the dining room and saw Billie-Jo on the patio floor covered in blood. She told the interviewer that she began to cry and her father rang for the ambulance. He then phoned Denise Lancaster, a near neighbour asking her to come over to the house. When she arrived, she sat with Charlotte and Annie.

The ambulance not having arrived, Sion Jenkins rung once more and said they needed paramedics to attend. Denise took Charlotte and Annie down to her house where they stayed. About half-an-hour later, her mother arrived at Denise's house together with Charlotte's other two small sisters. She and Annie told the policemen who had arrived that the gate was open.

The interviewer then asked Charlotte what made her notice that the garden gate was open. Charlotte replied that normally you would just see a brown gate closed. On that occasion she could clearly see the rabbit hutch behind the gate. She also confirmed that the gate was normally shut. This interview with Charlotte finished at 5:20 pm and lasted 90 minutes.

Annie's interview began at 5:35 pm and she was first asked about what happened to the side gate. Annie confirmed that Sion had closed it when they were going out. Unlike her sister, Charlotte, Annie had not noticed anything specific about the gate. When asked whether Billie-Jo had ever been left alone in the house before that occasion, she replied that she had and it was not the first time.

As they were leaving to go to the DIY store, Annie

said she had spoken to Billie-Jo. Whilst waiting in the hall, she could see Billie-Jo sitting on the floor near the patio doors and painting them. She said that Billie had said "Hello" to her and she had replied the same back to her. She, Charlotte and Sion walked out of the house.

Annie was then asked where her father was when she spoke to Billie. Her reply was that she was not sure. She thought he was with her but didn't know. Annie's interview concluded at 6:14 pm having lasted approximately 39 minutes in total.

What does emerge from these two interviews just 24 hours after the murder, is that the police were, even at this early stage of the investigation, convinced in their preliminary view, that Sion Jenkins himself must have been involved in what happened to Billie-Jo.

Both girls were asked about prowlers and other possible suspects and whether they had noticed anything suspicious. However, there appears to have been little interest shown in the answers given by these two girls. The children did attempt to open up avenues of questioning about other suspects, but the interviewers tended to turn these into cul-de-sacs.

These potential lines of enquiry were rapidly abandoned. Instead, the questions appeared to be focused exclusively on Sion Jenkins, and the suspicion that he must have been involved in Billie-Jo's death. Naturally, the children were not so naïve that they didn't recognise this. Observers of the case have suggested that some senior figures at Sussex Police appear to have compiled their own scenario of what happened on the day of the murder.

'Sion had murdered Billie-Jo while his two daughters were outside at the front of the house waiting by the car. He then quickly thought up the ruse of going to the DIY store for white spirit as a means of distancing himself from the crime scene'.

Hints of this theory are seen in the first questioning of

daughter, Charlotte.

Q: "At what point did you know you were going to the DIY store?"
A: "My Dad went down the stairs and he had the leather cloth to wipe the car but he didn't bring down the bucket. He said "Jump in" so he must have not brought the bucket because he remembered the white spirit."
Q: "At that point, what did you think you were going to do?"
A: "Clean the MG."
Q: "So, you didn't know you were going to the DIY store at that time?"
A: "No."

Elsewhere in Charlotte's interview, her replies reveal just how brief the first return to the house had really been.

A: "We went home and my Dad said 'Run and put your clarinet back'. When I came back down the stairs, my Dad said, 'Jump in'. We needed some white spirit because Annie wanted to paint and Billie was already painting, but just in case she got it anywhere."
Q: "When you went into the house, did only you get out of the car?"
A: "I think we all got out of the car, but Annie and Dad were waiting for me to come down so we could go and get the white spirit."
Q: "How many of you went to the front door, whether all of you went into the house or not?"
A: "My Dad opened the door. I can remember my Dad putting the keys on the mantlepiece. I can't remember where Annie was, though. I ran and put my clarinet in my room and came back down, and then my Dad realised that we needed the white spirit, so then we went to get it."
Q: "When you left to go to get the white spirit, who left the

house first?"
A: "I think it was me. I think Annie was waiting down by the MG. I think I went out first and then my Dad shut the door behind us with his door key because you can't shut the door without putting the key in."
Q: "Was there any time between when you left the house and when your Dad left the house?"
A: "No. I came out and he came out just after me and then shut the door."

At this point, Charlotte had already provided vital evidence about the overwhelming likelihood of an intruder having entered the house during their absence from it. When Annie was interviewed, she too was questioned about a possible interval between her and Charlotte leaving the house, and Sion doing so.

Q: "When you had spoken to Billie and Lotte had put her clarinet back, you and Lotte came down to the MG. How long was it before your Dad came out?"
A: "A few minutes, about two minutes, one minute."

This entire case hinged on this response and it is of vital importance. It would be referred to regularly throughout the prosecution's case at the third and final trials. This is because the question presupposes a time interval. More importantly, it is a leading question and Annie was intentionally being led by the interviewer.

The way the question was framed could have induced a particular and expected response. So, in the last question, Annie was asked "How long was it?" She instantly realises that her answer wasn't accurate, so she reduced the time period to "about two minutes, one minute".

All questions in a criminal context should have been asked 'neutrally'. The problem with 'leading questions' is that they produce misleading answers.

At the very end of Annie's first interview, the interviewer returned to the point in an attempt to clarify it.

Q; "Just before you went to the DIY store, you were standing by the MG with Lotte, is that right?"
A: "Yes."
Q: "Where was Dad then?"
A: "I think he was next to the Opel, next to our other car, but I'm not sure, I don't know."

The evidence on this one point that can be extracted from the interviewee is significant. On the one hand, Annie, in response to a leading question said that her father was in the house for "a few minutes". On the other hand, in answer to other questions, she had answered at different points as follows:
"We all just walked out",
"Then Dad said, "Come on" so I just went with him",
"I think he might have been behind me",
"I think he was with me as well but I don't know, I can't remember", and
"We went outside and I think Dad was outside with us as well".

At the end of Annie's first interview, the interviewer asked the crucial question:
Q: "Was he (Sion) in the house with Billie at any time?"
A: "No. I was in the house and I saw her."

Interviewing is a difficult art to master, and Annie was not an easy interviewee. It was Annie whose answer "it was a few minutes, about two minutes, one minute" before her father followed her and Charlotte outside, that provided the platform on which the prosecution case was being built against Sion Jenkins. The only way the prosecution could take the case forward was by eliciting extra detail from

Annie about this supposed time-gap. Ironically, all the prosecution had established was there was no time gap at all. Annie reiterated that she, Lotte and her father "all left the house at about the same time".

THE CASE AGAINST SION JENKINS

Sion Jenkins' first informal interview with the police took place during the evening of Saturday 15 February, the day of the murder of Billie-Jo. This was at the home of neighbour, Denise Lancaster, and was conducted by PC Darren Bruce, one of the first officers to arrive at the scene in the afternoon.

This interview lasted from 6:00 to 9:00 pm and was followed by a further interview at Battle Police Station on the Sunday evening 16 February. The post-mortem of Billie-Jo took place during the morning of Monday 17 February. In the afternoon, Sion and Lois made the formal identification of their foster-daughter. The following day was Tuesday 18 February, and Sion and Lois attended Hastings police station in the morning to make a public appeal regarding the murder. In the afternoon, Sion attended Battle police station for further interviews which lasted into the evening.

This was followed on Wednesday 19 February with a further all-day interview session. Finally on Thursday 20 February, following another interview, Sion Jenkins signed his 42 pages of statements. On Friday 21 February, Detective Superintendent Jeremy Paine who was leading the investigation, received a faxed letter from Adrian Wain, the forensic scientist working for the police. The text read as follows:

"A preliminary examination of Sion Jenkins' trousers and jacket has shown that there are many tiny specks of blood on the lower left leg of the trousers, and the lower

left sleeve of the jacket. These spots are typical of those which I would expect to find following an impact onto a surface wet with blood. The size of the spots also indicate that the force of the impact was considerable, and that the wearer was close to it".

Wain confirmed that the blood had been tested at the forensic laboratory in Wetherby, Yorkshire, and it had proved to be that of Billie-Jo. Even though this letter clearly stated that it was a preliminary examination, the insinuation was clearly made that Sion Jenkins was the killer.

On Monday 24 February, Sion Jenkins was arrested on suspicion of the murder of Billie-Jo and was kept in police custody. However, at lunchtime on Tuesday 25 February, this evidence was put to Jenkins. Then at 6:00 pm, he was released without charge. He went to stay with his parents in Aberystwyth in Wales. However, on Tuesday 15 March 1997, Sion Jenkins was re-arrested and charged with the murder of Billie-Jo and remanded to prison. On 26 March, Sion Jenkins was given bail on the condition that he resided with his parents to await trial.

THE POLICE EVIDENCE AGAINST JENKINS

More than 150 microscopic bloodspots were found on Jenkins' jacket. This was consistent only with him having been the attacker. He had up to three minutes alone in the house with Billie-Jo in which he could have killed her. He made a bogus journey to a DIY store taking an unnecessarily long route to buy white spirit which he did not need. The purpose of this journey was to establish an alibi.

It was contended that Sion Jenkins murdered his foster daughter in the time period between arriving home from collecting Charlotte from her clarinet lesson and then leaving to go to the DIY store. His daughters Annie and Charlotte were outside the front of the house waiting by Sion's car when he committed the act. During interviews with the police, Jenkins stated that he did not go into the house at all, but waited outside with Annie while Charlotte went inside to drop off her clarinet in her room.

However, he admitted later that he did go into the house but didn't see Billie-Jo. It was speculated by police that he initially lied about not going into the house to distance himself from the crime scene. However, he changed his story because his statements made to the police differed from both of his daughters.

Jenkins said in his first 999 call to the ambulance service, and later in a statement to the police, that he had been away from the house for between 30 and 45 minutes. A reconstructed timed police drive to and from the DIY store took approximately 15 minutes. We were told that he simply drove to the store and back again, not going into the store or even getting out of his car.

How then, could he claim (twice) that the short car journey could take over half an hour? It would certainly appear that he was lying to give himself the longest possible alibi. The journey taken to the DIY store appeared to be a strange one, since there was an adequate supply of white spirit already stored in the house. Not surprisingly, police suspected that it had been entirely manufactured as a reason for Jenkins to distance himself from the crime scene and create an alibi.

This theory is further supported by the fact that he drove around the nearby Alexandra Park in a circle to extend the journey.

Jenkins told the second 999 operator that he had turned Billie-Jo over and placed her in the recovery position when he was asked. This was untrue because he did not do this and later even admitted it. Apart from this specific lie, ambulance paramedics at the scene observed that Jenkins had done nothing at all to try and help his foster daughter. He later claimed that the blood on his clothing was due to Billie-Jo exhaling onto him which suggested he believed she was still alive, which in itself appeared suspect. Police were also suspicious why, when he saw Billie-Jo's battered body, he spent time calming his other two daughters in the house, rather than calling an ambulance as soon as the body had been found, particularly if he really believed that she was still alive.

Jenkins' other observed behaviour raised suspicions. Ambulance paramedics attending the scene found it odd that Jenkins did not stay with Billie-Jo as they attended to her. Instead, he went to the front of the house and just sat in his MG car. Police suspect this was to provide an excuse if Billie-Jo's blood should be found in his car, in case he transferred it on his journey to the DIY store.

Regarding a possible motive for the killing, police suggested that the day of the murder had been a frustrating one for Sion Jenkins. There had been a series of petty mishaps and wasted journeys. According to Lois, his wife, he had argued with Billie-Jo earlier in the day. Did something Billie-Jo say or do trigger an outburst so violent that he bludgeoned her to death? There was no evidence of an intruder, and no apparent motive for anyone to kill Billie-Jo.

She had defence wounds from blows to her arms, but there were no indications of a struggle and nothing to suggest that she tried to run away from her attacker. Also, there was no evidence to suggest that she was the victim of a sexual assault. Whoever committed the act went straight to bludgeoning her in the head. They didn't bring a weapon with them, but they used one conveniently placed in the garden by daughter Annie after cleaning out the utility room. Jenkins was the only person in the family who knew it was there.

The crux of the case against Sion Jenkins was the

discovery of blood on his clothing. The prosecution's forensic experts argued that such blood spatter could only have occurred when the girl was attacked.

Jenkins' neighbour, Denise Lancaster, who had cradled Billie-Jo and wrapped her head in a towel, did not have any blood spatter on herself, and neither did the paramedics who had contact with Billie-Jo. In addition, Jenkins' claim that he had never seen the tent pegs before was clearly a lie.

There were also further examples of inconsistencies and confusion in his statements to the police. He had also made a series of jottings in which he had carefully annotated the events of the fateful day, placing everything in chronological order, and simply referring to himself as "S J". From the police point of view, this was evidence of a guilty man attempting to get his story right. In addition, there was nothing mentioned in Jenkins' statements that indicated that Billie-Jo had any signs of 'gasping or breathing'.

CHAPTER FOUR

THE FORENSIC EVIDENCE

EXTRACTS FROM BILLIE-JO' S POST-MORTEM REPORT.

This was performed on the morning of Sunday 16 February 1997, by Home Office pathologist, Dr Ian Hill. She was found to have died as the result of fatal blows to her head. She also had bruising and abrasions to her forearms and the back of one hand, which were described as 'defence wounds'. She had bruising around her wrists which appeared to be about one week old. The wounds to her head were described as 'random' but within close proximity to each other. These had been inflicted by an estimated nine blows. She had a broken nose with severe bruising to her left eye. She also had a 2" x 2" injury to her right forehead which had depressed her skull in an oval shape. She had four gaping lacerations, two of which revealed her fractured skull. This was described as "a bit like a shattered egg".

The lines of fracture had travelled down to both eyes, ear and nose. Billie-Jo's brain had been badly torn and lacerated during the attack. Fragments of skull and brain were found matted in her blood-stained dark brown hair. Dr Hill stated that it was probable that the injuries to the front of Billie-Jo's head were inflicted with the attacker standing in front of her, and those on the top of her head, caused while she was lying on the ground.

Even though she had suffered devastating injuries to her skull, it was determined that due to the size of the weapon and the number of blows inflicted, it was reasonable to assume that extreme force was not necessary to shatter the skull. The murder weapon, an 18-inch-long iron tent peg, was found to have blood on both ends of it. This suggests that it was probably wielded by being held in the middle rather than at one end. There were no fingerprints found on the weapon.

BLOOD PATTERN ANALYSIS

The identification of bloodstain patterns is, by its very nature subjective. However, it is underpinned by sound scientific principles. By applying these principles, the identification and interpretation of these patterns can be made sufficiently objective to be applied to the investigation of crime.

IMPACT SPATTER

This is the most common type of blood pattern encountered in forensic casework. It can be the result of a wide range of actions such as kicking, stamping, beating and punching, and also with shooting. The cause of an impact spatter is a force impacting directly into wet blood. This breaks the blood down into small droplets which can be of varying volume. These droplets are then dispersed radially from the site of impact, having various trajectories and velocities. As a general rule, the greater the force applied to the impact site, the smaller will be the average size of the droplets. A number of variable factors will affect the distance, direction and quantity of the blood spattered by an impact. These will include the amount of wet blood present at the impact site, the position of the impact site relative to the assailant, the shape and size of the weapon used, and the speed and angle of the weapon at the moment of impact.

Assuming that the blood droplets have the same initial velocity and trajectory, smaller droplets will travel less far than the larger ones, because of the effects of air resistance. Detailed examination of impact patterns can provide significant information to a criminal investigation. Recognising impact spatter allows for the identification of sites of attack, and the determination of the relative position of objects and people at a crime scene. The patterns may also offer information as to the nature of the impact that caused the spatter. More importantly, they can give an indication of the likelihood of blood staining being present at the scene. This helps to determine the significance of bloodstains found on a suspect's clothing.

When an assailant delivers a series of blows in a 'frenzied' attack, one of the tell-tale pieces of evidence is 'Cast Off' blood. This is blood from the victim which has been transferred from the victim to the weapon and is then dripped onto the shoulders or back of the assailant. This is essentially associated with the swinging of a weapon.

The size of droplets cast-off from a swinging weapon will depend on the shape of the weapon, the nature of its surface, the velocity with which it is swung and the amount of blood present on the victim. Short heavy weapons tend to be swung more slowly and in shorter arcs. As more force can usually be applied on the forward swing of a weapon, it is generally easier to generate cast-off when a weapon is swung in the forward direction.

For example, where an assailant bludgeons his victim with a heavy weapon, involving many blows a considerable spatter can be directed back towards the assailant, creating heavy spattering on his shirt or front clothing. However, it is also quite possible for the majority of spatter from a beating to be directed forwards or to the sides and away from the assailant. In situations where there have been numerous blows inflicted, it is likely that the assailant will be bloodstained to some extent. However, with a single or few blows, it may be that no blood at all is directed onto the assailant.

Source: 'Crime Scene to Court: The Essentials of Forensic Science'. Peter White (Ed). 2nd Edit. (Royal Society of Chemistry, Cambridge, 2004, Chapter 5).

THE MECHANICS OF HEAD INJURY

Common head injuries which may occur either singly or in combinations, are bruising or lacerations to the scalp. A bruise is a haemorrhage into tissues, whereas a laceration is a tear in tissue. There are also fractures of the skull which can be divided into those involving the vault which covers the upper and outer surfaces of the brain, or the base, on which the brain rests. These injuries may be caused by sharp weapons or by blunt force, and may be homicidal, suicidal or accidental in origin. The tissues of the scalp are comparatively dense and are lined internally by firm but very vascular fibrous tissue. Direct violence to the scalp which lies on the rigid vault of the skull results in a unique form of crushing between two hard objects. If the crush is of a minor nature, a contusion or bruise will be produced, and tracking of blood is likely to be slight in the dense connective tissue.

Since the scalp is held firmly over the skull, it is not unusual for the outer surface to reproduce the pattern of the weapon or object responsible for the violence. The skin will split when the compressive force is greater, the scalp being the classic place for lacerated wounds to be produced by blunt force because the skull is convex. With the application of greater force, the underlying skull will fracture. The skull is not uniformly solid, but is composed of two layers or tables of bones separated by spongy tissue. When struck, the skull will deform to some extent depending largely upon its age. A child's skull will bend before breaking, but since blood vessels will be torn in the process, head injury in children often shows a surprising degree of haemorrhage when compared with the relative lack of damage to the skull itself. Once the bounds of moulding are passed, the bone will break.

Usually, lines of stress fracture radiate from the point of contact, while that part of the skull struck is depressed, a situation almost exactly comparable with 'striking the shell of a hard-boiled egg'. These radiating fractures may damage blood vessels over a wide area. The membranes of the brain with their accompanying blood vessels, may be crushed or torn beneath a depressed fracture. More seriously, the brain itself may be lacerated either by the weapon causing the external injury, or by the fragments of bone that are forced inwards.

Source: Forensic Medicine for Lawyers, JK Mason, (Butterworth, Sevenoaks, 1983) Chapter 11.

The critical evidence in the Jenkins' case was essentially 'scientific'. Those who were present at the scene of Billie-Jo's murder submitted items of the clothing they had been wearing on Saturday 15 February 1997 for forensic testing. All of these items were examined by forensic scientist Adrian Wain at the forensic science laboratory in Lambeth, South London. The most revealing of these tests was microscopic examination of Sion Jenkins' clothing which identified a total of 158 bloodspots. These minute spots were distributed as follows:

79 On the lower right leg
4 Higher up the right leg.
2 On the left leg.
63 On Jenkins' fleece jacket.
10 On Jenkins' left shoe.

However, there were no cast-off drops found anywhere on Jenkins' clothing. Virtually all of these bloodspots were invisible to the naked eye. Specific areas from this bloodstained clothing were sent to the forensic laboratory at Wetherby in Yorkshire for DNA analysis.

This analysis confirmed that all the blood on the items submitted from Sion Jenkins was Billie-Jo's. These bloodspots were approximately the same size as those found on Billie-Jo's leggings. There was no blood found on the clothing from Jenkins' neighbour, Denise Lancaster, or either of the two paramedics who attended Billie-Jo at the murder scene. There was no broad area of bloodstaining on Jenkins' clothing which there would have been if he had cradled Billie-Jo in his arms.

Wain asserted that there was nothing mentioned in Sion Jenkins' statements made to the police which could explain the presence of these bloodspots found on his clothing. Wain's personal supposition was that there was only one explanation for the presence of the bloodspots, and the supposition was that Jenkins himself had killed Billie-Jo.

Wain further stated that Billie-Jo had been bludgeoned at close range and that the blows inflicted were considerable. He further suggested that using the weapon identified, would have caused larger drops to shoot forward. This would have created a fine spray of smaller droplets which would go upwards and backwards towards the assailant since these smaller droplets would not travel far. This suggested that the assailant was in very close contact with the victim at the time of the attack.

Significantly, Wain emphasised that the range and distribution of the bloodspots on Jenkins' jacket and trousers were typical of what one would expect to find, if Jenkins had been the assailant, leaning forward and attacking Billie-Jo with the tent peg, impacting a surface of wet blood.

In this scenario, the first blow delivered would not produce a spray, since there would be no exposed blood on the victim's skull at that time. If, however, subsequent blows were aimed at or near the area of first impact, then sprays would occur.

From his statements to the police, it would appear that Sion Jenkins had leant over Billie-Jo and had noticed what he described as a 'bubble of blood' at her nose. According to the post-mortem report, there was blood found in Billie-Jo's airways. Her lungs were described as being 'hyper- inflated', meaning that they were fully extended and air was trapped within them.

Given these conditions, it was believed by Sion Jenkins' defence team that Billie-Jo might, at some point, have exhaled a fine 'bloody mist' over Sion as he leant over her. The 'bubble of blood' does provide an indication of how this may have occurred.

The key question here is: "Was the blood found on Sion Jenkins' clothing, caused by impact spatter as suggested by Adrian Wain, or by exhalation spray?"

It would appear that at this early stage, the prosecution had not even considered the possibility that the blood spots found on Jenkins' clothing could have been caused by anything other than that he was the assailant.

It was only at the beginning of April 1997 when the defence disclosed their own forensic reports to the prosecution, that they became aware of the defence's argument which ran contrary to Wain's findings.

The defence forensic reports were compiled by two experts from Imperial College, London, Duncan MacKirdy and Mark Webster, together with an independent report submitted by consultant neurosurgeon John Sinar. In his report, Sinar, an expert in head injuries, explained the differences between a closed and open head wound. In the former, death can be rapid due to intercranial pressure, being unable to be released. In the latter, the victim can remain alive relatively longer.

The amount of blood present at the murder scene indicated that Billie-Jo's heart must still have been pumping blood around the body. Therefore, death was not instantaneous. This in itself, illustrates that Billie-Jo must still have been alive after the attack on her.

However, Sinar did state that it was difficult to be absolutely certain when death did occur. Even after serious head injuries, 'breathing' can still continue for a time. He estimated that Billie-Jo may have survived for 15-20 minutes post-attack.

In addition, respiration could have been produced by moving Billie-Jo's body.

Duncan MacKirdy, joint-author of the defence forensic report, stated that he would not have expected the bloodspots found on Sion Jenkins' clothing to have been produced by impact spatter and to also be of similar size. He, together with Mark Webster, suggested that the pattern of staining similar to that produced on Sion's clothing, could only have been produced by 'exhalation'.

To counter this assertion, the prosecution maintained it would have been necessary for Billie-Jo to have inhaled a large amount of air in order for her to have expired the blood drops found on Jenkins' clothing.

Dr Ian Hill, the Home Office pathologist maintained that Billie-Jo would have been unable to make any vigorous breathing movements given her dying state.

He also added that had she in fact, expelled blood in the manner suggested by the defence, then someone in close proximity to her, like Jenkins would have certainly noted her breathing.

In the event, Sion did not report such movement in any of his statements to police. In conclusion, Hill considered the defence theory' was a "remote possibility that would be discarded".

One of the prosecution's expert forensic scientists, John McAughey, was an authority on the measurement of air flow. Having carried out experiments, he recorded that for Billie-Jo to have expelled blood droplets with sufficient force to create a spray, this would require approximately 2.7 litres of air, representing a peak air flow of between 50 and 55 litres per minute or approximately 80% of Billie-Jo's total lung capacity.

This flow is the rate at which air comes out of the body, and is measured in litres of air per minute. Peak flow is the fastest rate of respiration without 'undue effort'.

Normal breathing occurs at a rate of approximately 30 litres per minute. Maximum air flow requires about 70 litres per minute. The thrust of the prosecution's evidence to counter the defence's exhalation theory, was that Billie-Jo would have required the lung capacity and fitness of a track-athlete to generate the air flow required to produce the kind of blood spray discovered on Sion Jenkins' fleece jacket.

To counter this assertion by the prosecution, the defence produced another expert witness, Professor Douglas. He argued that what caused the 50 and 55 litres per minute was not the amount of air generated, but the flow of air. He remarked that 55 litres was close to twice the normal lung capacity, but would in fact, be 'a relatively low-peak flow'.

In order for the prosecution's theory (that Sion Jenkins killed Billie-Jo), to be sustained, they had to be able to demonstrate conclusively that it was virtually impossible for Billie-Jo to have still been alive when Jenkins discovered her, and that it was equally impossible for her to have 'expirated' blood onto Jenkins's clothing. The only possible explanation for the blood on the clothing was that it had been caused by impact spatter only.

At Jenkins' first trial in 1998, Professor David Denison from Imperial College, London, reported that if

Billie-Jo's airways contained blood (as in all likelihood it did after trauma) and she had breathed out, that would result in the kind of spray seen on Sion Jenkins' clothing.

He further argued that a single exhalation could indeed have produced all the bloodspots found on Sion's clothing. Moreover, the exhalation could well have been brief; passive, inaudible and invisible, and could even have occurred after death. However, Denison also pointed out that there must have been a blockage in Billie-Jo's upper airways.

He further suggested that when the blockage was eased, the build-up of air trapped in the lungs, would have been released under pressure, creating the exhalation spray. The foundations of the scientific defence against the murder charge were laid by both Professor David Denison and his colleague Professor Robert Schroter from Sheffield University.

At a legal conference before Sion Jenkins' Second Appeal in 2004, defence leading counsel, Clare Montgomery QC, told Denison that in order to demonstrate to even 'the most sceptical court audience' that the human body could behave as the defence scientific experts had asserted, they would have to employ real blood.

To facilitate this, Denison and Schroter used stored hospital blood past its sell-by date. Together, the two experts conducted a number of experiments centred on blood expiration. These experiments became increasingly important in demonstrating that the defence theory of the bloodspots (expiration spray) was not only viable in itself, but was an overwhelmingly more feasible interpretation of the available information that the prosecution's theory of impact spatter.

In effect, these experiments transformed the way in which forensic science works in this specific speciality. However, there was growing concern among the 'scientific community' involved in this case, that Billie-Jo's post-mortem should have been conducted differently.

In particular, it was expressed that so little was undertaken to preserve vital material that could have enabled the case to be clarified more clearly. For example, John Sinar, the consultant neurosurgeon commented that "It is unfortunate that the brain was not removed and preserved for later microscopic examination".

In fact, all that was preserved were four small sections of the lung, one from each lobe, which were taken for histological examination.

It was not until these samples were examined by Professors Helen Whitwell and Christopher Milroy, who together carried out histological work for the defence, that it became clear that the lungs were inflated, confirming that there must have been a blockage.

On Tuesday 15 June, 2004, in the Royal Brompton Hospital's pathology department, a small group of scientists gathered to examine the preserved slides of sections of Billie-Jo's lungs. It was a member of this group, Professor Nicholson, who made the observation that would transform the whole case.

Billie-Jo had Pulmonary Interstitial Emphysema (PIE). This occurs when someone is making violent attempts to breathe but the main airways are blocked. As a result, the lining is torn, the air cannot escape, and will be forced under pressure into the linings of the lungs.

Billie-Jo did not suffer from any respiratory disease, nor do severe head injuries cause PIE. It is only seen in healthy people if their lungs have come under pressure in a variety of ways. This can be through being held in an arm lock, strangulation, smothering or drowning.

This discovery proved two things. Firstly, that Billie-Jo did not die instantly because there had been time for these physiological changes to have taken place. Secondly, that she had suffered a blockage of her airway. Sion Jenkins' first appeal against conviction in 1999 rejected

Professor Denison's evidence precisely because it was predicted on the basis that there had been an upper airway blockage.

At this appeal, Lord Justice Kennedy emphasised in his judgment that there was no evidence of any blockage. The evidence of the Home Office pathologist, Dr Ian Hill, had been controversial at the time of the first appeal. This was mainly because he was giving opinions about Billie-Jo's post-mortem that he had never experienced before and had made notes which supported his theory.

In dismissing Jenkins' first appeal, the judges had relied too heavily on Dr Hill's testimony. The further scientific work had now proved him wrong. As a result, the entire perspective of the case had dramatically changed. This resulted in further analysis of the scientific evidence for the prosecution being undertaken by a senior Home Office pathologist, Dr Nay Cary. He developed a new strategy arguing that the lung tissue slides did not reveal evidence of PIE in Billie-Jo. He maintained that the linings in the lungs could have been a bubble artifact which is a product of the histological process itself, which can occur during the process of preparing slides from the lung sample.

A second strand of the prosecution's case was developed by Dr Jeremy Skepper at Cambridge University. He conducted a further examination of the surviving bloodspots from the samples of Sion Jenkins' clothing, using electron microscopy, and detected what he termed white spots within the bloodspots themselves.

These, according to Dr Skepper, could have been particles of skin which could have come from damaged tissue on Billie-Jo's scalp. The prosecution's strategy at the first retrial in 2005, was two-fold. First, to reject the defence theory of PIE, and the expirated spray, and, second, to construct its own case comprised of the presence of what became known as the 'white inclusions' found within the bloodspots themselves. This, they maintained, would prove that Sion Jenkins had violently attacked Billie-Jo because particles of skin as well as blood had landed on Jenkins' clothing.

Sion's legal team had assembled a team of leading scientists to assess the scientific aspects of the prosecution's revised case. There was no doubt amongst the defence scientists that the prosecution's new stance on PIE was misconceived.

Three of the world's authorities in this specialist field of medicine, Professors David Denison, Andrew Nicholson and William Travis from New York, each examined and concluded that the "evidence for the presence of PIE in the tissue slides was absolutely unequivocal".

These three defence scientists found the 'white inclusions' argument to be specious. The 158 bloodspots found on Jenkins' clothing amounted to merely one drop of blood roughly $1/2^{th}$ of a millilitre. This was, according to Professor Denison an almost "infinitesimally small" proportion of the total blood lost by Billie-Jo as a result of the attack on her.

To place 158 microscopic bloodspots into proportion, a vigorous 'sneeze' will normally generate around 20,000 tiny droplets of mucus, saliva and phlegm. This is about 100 times as many as the number of bloodspots found on Sion Jenkins' clothing. In the circumstances of this particular attack, it is only to be expected that the particles of blood would contain elements of skin and other bodily material.

There were also other considerations to take into account. Billie-Jo's airways would certainly have been damaged by the forced insertion of the plastic bin liner into her left nostril. The cruciform plate (or ethmoid bone) lies in the floor of the skull and forms the roof of the nasal cavity, and it separates the interior of the nose from the brain. In Billie-Jo's case, this was fractured. As a result, it would not be surprising that microscopic fragments of skin, bone and even brain itself, would all be present in her expirated blood.

Having reviewed the evidence, another defence scientist, Laurence Watkins, determined that it was unlikely that death would have been instantaneous, and that the brainstem reflexes which included breathing and coughing would have continued to be present at the time Sion Jenkins arrived at the murder scene.

The respiratory function is "One of the basic brain stem reflexes, and one of the last to disappear during the process of dying. Forceable expiration may not always be loud enough to be noted".

Robert Schroter, Professor of Biological Mechanics at Imperial College, London took over much of the defence scientific work at Sion Jenkins' second re-trial in 2005, together with colleague Julian Hunt. Schroter conducted experiments in ambient air currents to establish scientifically, how blood droplets would travel in the atmosphere and environmental conditions that would have been expected on the Jenkins' patio in Hastings.

They concluded that droplets expelled by Billie-Jo would have landed on Sion Jenkins' clothing. This evidence was also examined by Joseph Slemko, an experienced Canadian police officer, who was gaining an international reputation as a forensic consultant in the field of bloodstain pattern evidence. He concluded that the pattern of bloodstaining on Sion Jenkins' fleece jacket was consistent only with the blood being expirated from a blood contaminated airway.

In order for the patterns on the clothing to be created, Sion Jenkins would have to be in a crouching, semi-kneeling position with the right side and right lower trouser leg exposed to the blood source, and with his torso twisted right and lowered to expose his inner chest area. This was a position that was inconsistent with Sion being the assailant, but consistent with him positioning himself to examine Billie-Jo.

Slemko also added that the prosecution theory that the pattern had been created by impact spatter, was highly improbable. At the first re-trial of Sion Jenkins (which began in April, 2005) Dr Ian Hill, the pathologist retained by the prosecution, had retired. He was replaced by Dr Nat Cary, a Senior Home Office pathologist.

Dr Jeremy Skepper, from the Department of Human Biology at Cambridge University, had been retained by the prosecution. He conducted further examination of the surviving bloodspots from Jenkins' clothing, using electron microscopy, and he detected white specks within the bloodspots themselves. He stated that they could have been particles of skin from damaged scalp tissue from Billie-Jo's skull.

The defence argument was they were also consistent with tissue from the inside of Billie-Jo's nostril. Previously, Dt Hill had insisted that he had examined Billie-Jo's nose as part of a routine procedure but he had not seen signs of any injury.

Leading defence counsel, Christopher Sallen QC, pointed out that in all the post-mortem reports, there was "no reference to his having examined the nostrils". Hill's explanation was "that you don't normally put it in the notes". Sallen further pointed out that there were references to all other areas of Billie-Jo's body in his notes, but nothing at all about his examination of the nose. However, Hill had insisted that it was normal procedure for pathologists to undertake nasal examination but not to record them in the post-mortem reports.

Photographs taken of Billie-Jo's nose at post-mortem did show one nostril blocked with crusted dried blood. The other nostril also had a plastic bin liner inserted into it under force. Defence Counsel, Christopher Sallen QC, took the jury through the photographs of the crime scene and was able to demonstrate that the scene-of-crime work had not been particularly thorough. Many bloodspots over the patio area and inside the house had not been taken into consideration by the prosecution. For example, there were two trellises outside and one had not been removed, so the walls behind had not been examined. In addition, many spots at some greater distance from the body of Billie-Jo than the main concentration of spots, had never been examined. The location and size of these spots indicated a dynamic attack. There was a high probability that the assailant would have intercepted a lot of blood spatter. There was no evidence of this on Sion Jenkins' clothing.

There was another vital piece of evidence that was totally ignored – a clearly visible footprint on the patio. Crime investigators globally would have regarded this as "gold standard evidence".

Billie-Jo had swept the patio that afternoon, so the footprint could not have been present earlier. It appeared to be the print of a male wearing boots with patterned soles. It would have been a routine forensic procedure to match this print to a particular boot. This footprint did not match Sion Jenkins nor any other member of the household. Also, it did not match any member of the emergency services attending the scene or Jenkins' neighbour, Denise Lancaster.

On the face of it, it would certainly appear that potentially vital evidence had simply been ignored. It was clear that Billie-Jo had defended herself against her assailant because defensive wounds were found on her body. Significantly, these wounds do suggest that her assailant had been in different positions when he attacked Billie-Jo, and could have shed blood himself.

However, when questioned by defence counsel, the scene-of-crime officer confirmed that no DNA checks had been made on the blood spots far away from the main scene, to ascertain whether they were those of Billie-Jo or the assailant. Regrettably, this evidence was lost due to poor preservation and examination protocols.

What the prosecution had purported to have discovered was that bloodspots on Sion's clothing contained not just Billie-Jo's blood, but also particles of skin, tissue and bone, together with specks of paint and fragments of metal. The obvious insinuation was that the prosecution was seeking to establish that minute traces of the murder weapon itself (the tent-peg) had been found on Sion Jenkins' clothing. The prosecution regarded this as dramatic new evidence. However, taken in context, the situation turned out to be rather different.

In retrospect, the prosecution at Sion Jenkins' original trial in 1998, had argued that the microscopic bloodspots found on Jenkins' clothing were compelling evidence that proved Sion Jenkins was guilty of the murder of Billie-Jo. Then at the first re-trial in April, 2005, the prosecution was launched on the basis that it was the 'white inclusions' that provided the scientific underpinning of the prosecution's case against Sion Jenkins.

Progressing to the second re-trial in October 2005, the prosecution was continued on the basis that guilt could be proven, not by the invisible bloodspots themselves, nor by the 'white inclusions' at the centre of some of those spots, but by even more microscopic fragments that lay, within the 'white inclusions' within the invisible spots. After all this, fragments of human material, whether bone, brain matter or anything else, were not actually present.

However, what the prosecution did discover instead, were fragments of metal, which certainly raised the temperature, however briefly. They asked the question, "Could this have come from the murder weapon itself?" However, this was short-lived as there was no connection between the piece of metal and the murder weapon. Wherever it originated, it was not the tent peg.

This was the vital evidence the jury did not hear at the original trial in 1998. At the start of Sion Jenkins' first trial in 1998, the defence presented an expert report from John Sinar, consultant neurosurgeon at Middlesborough General Hospital. He also presented a second report, in which he emphasised a number of very significant points.

Firstly, that patients with open-head wounds, will often survive for a period of time (around 20 minutes being feasible). He also stressed that it was not normal for patients to die immediately. Secondly, that the pooling of blood on the patio, strongly supported the theory that Billie-Jo had not died instantly following the attack. Thirdly, that unconscious patients will exhale mucus or blood when being moved. Fourthly, that the exhaled blood or mucus will spray medical staff.

All these significant points support the contention that Sion Jenkins could well have been sprayed with blood as he tended to Billie-Jo on his discovery. Sinar added two further significant points. First, that Sion had no brain matter on his clothing. This would certainly have been anticipated had he been the assailant. Second, that there was no blood staining on Sion's thighs which strongly suggests that he was in a crouching position when the spray landed on him. This also supports the view that he was tending to her and not attacking her.

All the evidence which was disclosed by the defence to the prosecution, was served before the first trial commenced, and has stood the test of time.

CHAPTER FIVE

TRIALS AND APPEALS

Sion Jenkins was charged with the murder of his foster-daughter, Billie-Jo, in March 1997 and stood trial at Lewes Crown Court, where he was convicted and sentenced to life imprisonment in July 1998. In 1999 he appealed against his conviction but it was dismissed. Then in May 2003, the Criminal Cases Review Commission (CCRC) referred his case back to the Appeal Court.

In 2004, the second appeal was upheld, but it was ordered that Jenkins face a re-trial. The following year (2005) saw Jenkins face two re-trials, the first in July which resulted in a hung jury, and the prosecution calling for a further re-trial which was ordered by the court. This began in October and ended in February 2006 when once again the jury failed to reach a verdict.

Consequently, Jenkins was formally acquitted of the murder of Billie-Jo. The following timeline of the legal proceedings against Sion Jenkins described how the evidence differed in each of the trials and subsequent appeals.

FIRST TRIAL 1998

This first trial was centred essentially upon the forensic evidence – the bloodstains found on Jenkins' clothing. He was found guilty by a unanimous verdict and sentences to life imprisonment. The jury at this first trial did not hear about Jenkins' lying on his CV or evidence of previous violent conduct. His daughters, Annie and Charlotte, were not called to give evidence for the defence.

FIRST APPEAL 1999

This was based on two premises. Firstly, new forensic evidence and secondly, the fact that Jenkins' daughters did not testify at the original trial which placed the defence at a distinct disadvantage. It was asserted that the girls' statements to the police had been adversely influenced by their mother's false reporting to the police. The appeal was dismissed and the original conviction was upheld.

SECOND APPEAL 2004

The Criminal Cases Review Commission (CCRC) investigated Jenkins' case, and heard fresh forensic evidence from the defence which had been rejected during the first appeal in 1999. Forensic witnesses for the defence claimed that the bloodstaining on Sion Jenkins' clothing could have originated from a rare medical condition which would have caused pressure to build up in Billie-Jo's lungs. It was submitted that this condition had caused Billie-Jo to breath out blood involuntarily.

As a result of this new evidence, the CCRC referred the case back to the court of appeal in May 2003. The appeal court agreed that this alternative explanation made the original conviction of Sion Jenkins unsafe. In 2004, the second appeal was upheld but Jenkins was ordered to face a re-trial, and was granted bail in the interim period.

THE FIRST RE-TRIAL JULY 2005

The defence's forensic experts submitted that the microscopic blood spray could have been released from Billie-Jo's injured airways when Sion Jenkins moved her. After hours of deliberating, the jury could not arrive at a majority verdict. This resulted in the prosecution insisting that a second re-trial was necessary and the court ordered this.

THE SECOND RE-TRIAL OCTOBER 2005

The prosecution stated that the jury would need to decide whether the blood found on Jenkins' clothing got there when he attacked her, or when he discovered her body and moved her. This second and final trial resulted in the jury, once again, being unable to reach a majority verdict. Consequently, on 9 February, 2006, Sion Jenkins was acquitted and declared not guilty.

The Crown Prosecution Service (CPS) indicated that no further re-trials of Jenkins would be instigated. Sion Jenkins became the first man in British criminal history to be acquitted after being tried three times for the same crime.

THE FIRST TRIAL

At Jenkins' first trial at Lewes Crown Court in June 1998, the prosecution revealed that 158 bloodstains had been found on the jacket, trousers and shoes of Sion Jenkins. They submitted that these were the result of impact spatter from his attack on Billie-Jo. These bloodstains had the appearance of a fine spray, and two prosecution experts stated that the appearance and distribution of the resultant pattern was consistent with the prosecution assertion that Sion Jenkins was the assailant. Both of these experts agreed that it was "typical of the fine 'back-spatter' one would find on an assailant when a weapon 'impacted' on an already 'bloodied'' surface". In response to this assertion, the defence called on two scientific experts who stated that the evidence was not consistent with Jenkins being the assailant.

Sion Jenkins claimed that any blood found on his clothing was the direct result of his trying to help Billie-Jo when he discovered her. However, the prosecution countered this suggestion by stating that similar staining had not been found on the clothing of both of the paramedics who attended Billie-Jo, nor on the clothing of neighbour, Denise Lancaster, who had tried to save Billie-Jo.

In the 'Notice of Alibi', Sion's daughters, Annie and Charlotte, were named as defence witnesses. John Haines, junior counsel at a 'Plea and Direction' hearing in December 1997 (prior to the opening of the first trial) stated that a live video link would be required at the court to enable the two girls to give their evidence via a live TV link.

Annie and Charlotte had been with Sion at the critical time and therefore they would automatically have been called to give evidence. However, on 10 February 1998, a lawyer from the Crown Prosecution Service (CPS) drew Jenkins' solicitor's attention to police officers' reports which detailed conversations they had held with Lois Jenkins, Sion's then wife.

These had indicated that her two daughters were, in fact, going to change their evidence. In the light of this revelation, the defence team and lead defence counsel Anthony Scrivener QC, faced a significant dilemma.

What should the defence do about the children's evidence? Had they actually changed their evidence, and if so, why had it changed and what were they now saying?

The obvious course of action would be to ask the girls directly. However, neither Scrivener nor any of the defence legal team were allowed to do this. Their mother, Lois Jenkins, had refused permission for them to be interviewed.

As a result of this, Scrivener consulted a leading clinical psychologist, Dr Valerie Mellor, to prepare a report for the defence. However, to complicate matters further, she too was prevented from speaking to the children. She did prepare her report on the basis of the documentary material available to her, which was essentially the children's video interviews with the police, and accompanying police reports.

Her opinion was that it was "wholly inappropriate" that the debriefing of the children by investigating police officers had in fact, taken place at all. She considered this to amount to "tarnishing the evidence of these witnesses".

Mellor criticised Sussex Police in four distinct respects. The investigating officers had carried out the debriefing themselves instead of employing trained therapists or counsellors. If the girls were to be told anything, then this should have been restricted to the bare minimum. What in fact they were actually told went way beyond this. As a result, the children could be led to change their original accounts in order to please their mother, the police themselves or to accept other' information at face value.

If the meeting with the girls was to be held at all, then it should have been properly recorded. In fact, it appears there was no attempt to make any kind of contemporaneous records. Even though the *Memorandum of Good Practice of 1992* did not strictly apply to such meetings, nevertheless, its guidelines would be important for situations around child witnesses.

In this respect, Dr Mellor concluded that the Code of Conduct accompanying the Memorandum had been breached in a number of respects. In concluding her report, Dr Mellor felt that the children may well have been influenced to think in a negative way about their father or they may have reacted by feeling over protective towards Sion Jenkins. Whichever it was, it was going to affect the reliability of their recollection. The police actions had encouraged them to think differently about their father. As a result, any evidence they could give would be "tarnished".

Armed with Mellor's report, the defence submitted that the trial could not now take place. Scrivener submitted that it must have been obvious to the police from the video interviews that Annie and Charlotte were crucial defence witnesses.

The video interviews when closely analysed provided conclusive proof of Sion Jenkins' innocence. However, if the defence were to put forward the video evidence as a crucial part of its case and run the risk of calling the children, ignorant of what their changes consisted of, together with Lois Jenkins' reports made to the police, the children's evidence could prove very damaging to the defence case.

Where the inevitable result of conduct on the part of the police was to undermine the evidence of crucial alibi witnesses, Scrivener concluded that such conduct was so seriously wrong that it amounted to an interference with the administration of justice. This would also constitute a contempt of court.

The trial judge, Mr Justice Gage, heard the abuse of process arguments from both sides on the first day of the trial. On the following day (4 June 1998) he delivered his written judgment: "The fact that the children were asking questions which require some answers". He pointed out that the police then sought advice about what they should do. Although this advice may not have been completely followed, there is no evidence that what they did was done in bad faith'. Consequently, he ruled that there had been no abuse of process and concluded that nothing in Scrivener's arguments persuaded him that Sion Jenkins would be unable to have a fair trial.

In order for the prosecution's theory (that Sion Jenkins killed Billie-Jo) should succeed, they had to be able to conclusively demonstrate that it was not possible for Billie-Jo to have still been alive when Jenkins found her. In addition, they also had to show that it was not possible for her to have expirated blood onto Jenkins' clothing, and that it had been the result of impact spatter.

One of the crucial prosecution points which underpinned the scientific evidence, was Jenkins' reluctance to put on his fleece jacket when he and his wife Lois, were leaving the home of neighbour Denise Lancaster in the evening of the day of the killing. In regard to this, the prosecution argued that Jenkins felt uncomfortable wearing this jacket because he knew it was contaminated with Billie-Jo's blood.

At trial, the prosecution argued that Sion had a fit of temper, picked up the tent peg and bludgeoned Billie-Jo to death. The problems of the day had rankled him: Billie-Jo's rudeness, the dispute between Annie and Billie-Jo as to who would get the household job, together with Sion's unexpected chore of having to take Charlotte's friend home after their clarinet lesson. All these factors, the prosecution suggested had combined to create a day of mounting frustration for Jenkins.

By the time Billie-Jo exasperated him still more with her careless painting and playing loud music, he could tolerate no more and just cracked. It was in essence, a crime carried out in a moment of rage. However, all this supposition really amounted to circumstantial evidence, the real critical evidence was predominantly scientific.

The defence case rested on the argument that someone else was responsible for the murder of Billie-Jo. In addition, it was submitted that the case had not been investigated thoroughly and that vital leads had been ignored. According to defence leading counsel, Anthony Scrivener QC, it was a "murder inquiry which had lost its way".

With regard to Jenkins' reactions to the attack on Billie-Jo and his inability to deal adequately with the aftermath, Scrivener called Professor Michael Trimble, a consultant psychiatrist, who gave evidence of the extent to which we are all susceptible to the effects of shock in the aftermath of traumatic events.

Trimble felt that the inexplicable aspects of Sion's conduct (his alleged failure to tend to Billie-Jo satisfactorily, or to act on routine instructions of the ambulance operator) could all be straightforwardly explained by the fact that he was in deep shock. However, to rebut this suggestion, the prosecution argued that the notes Sion Jenkins had made during police interviews were intricate and detailed, and demonstrated that there was no question of shock having affected his memory.

In his summing up to the jury, the judge, Mr Justice Gage, compressed the case for the jury to consider into a series of questions:

"What was Billie-Jo's state when the defendant returned to the house?"
"Was she dead, or may she have still been alive? If so, in what state?"
"Was she capable of breathing at all?"
"What did he see and do in relation to Billie-Jo when he arrived back home?"
"Are you sure that the spots of blood on his clothes *must have* resulted from a fine spray, generated by his striking the blood wet surface of Billie-Jo's head with the tent peg?"

"May it have been caused by 'exhalation' of breath causing those blood droplets when he discovered her?"

On 2 July, 1998, Jenkins was convicted by a unanimous verdict, despite the jury being told by the judge that a majority alone would be enough for a conviction. He was sentenced to life imprisonment. However, on 21 December, 1998, Jenkins was granted leave to appeal his conviction.

THE FIRST APPEAL

A date was set for Sion Jenkins' first appeal which began at the Royal Courts of Justice in the Strand, London on 30 November 1999. Jenkins' defence counsel, Anthony Scrivener, QC put forward a number of grounds of appeal on behalf of Jenkins.

There had been an abuse of process when the police debriefed the children and as a result, the original trial judge Mr Justice Gage, had been wrong not to allow Scrivener's original pre-trial application and stop the trial.

Another ground was what became known as the 'confusion issue'. This involved arguments at the first trial concerning the volume of air that Billie-Jo would have required in her lungs to expel the blood spray.

There were then misunderstandings surrounding the evidence concerning lung capacity and air flow. Scrivener also asked the court to receive the new evidence of Professor David Denison. Professor Denison's evidence was rejected precisely because it was 'predicted' on the basis that there had been an upper airway blockage. At this appeal, Lord Justice Kennedy emphasised in his judgement that there "was no evidence of any blockage".

Case Name: R v Jenkins (Sion David Charles)

SMITH BERNAL

Case No: 98/4720/W3

IN THE COURT OF APPEAL
(CRIMINAL DIVISION)

Royal Courts of Justice
Strand, London, WC2A 2LL

Date: 21st December 1999

Before:

LORD JUSTICE KENNEDY

MR JUSTICE DYSON

and

MR JUSTICE PENRY-DAVEY

- - - - - - - - - - - - - - - - - - - -

Regina

- v -

SION JENKINS

- - - - - - - - - - - - - - - - - - - -

Handed down judgment of Smith Bernal Reporting Ltd
180 Fleet Street, London EC4A 2HG
Tel No: 0171 421 4040 Fax No: 0171 831 8838
(Official Shorthand Writers to the Court)

- - - - - - - - - - - - - - - - - - - -

MR ANTHONY SCRIVENER QC & **MR JOHN HAINES** appeared on behalf of the Appellant
MR CAMDEN PRATT QC & **MR A GARDNER** appeared on behalf of the Crown Prosecution)

- - - - - - - - - - - - - - - - - - - -

JUDGMENT
(As Approved by the Court)

- - - - - - - - - - - - - - - - - - - -

CONCLUSIONS

151: "We have already expressed our conclusions in relation to the first four issues which we identified at the beginning of this judgment. Even if we had decided in relation to the 'Confusion Issue' standing alone, without reference to further evidence, the mistakes which we there identified could be said to render the conviction unsafe, the fact is that at the request of the appellant we have now received fresh evidence, and in our judgment each ground of appeal does now fall to be determined in the light of all of the evidence. Mr Scrivener submitted otherwise, but we reject that submission which as he concedes, is devoid of authoritative support. The fresh evidence has left no room for doubt as to the distinction between minute volume and peak flow, and as to the positions occupied by each of the experts, but it has gone far further than that. We do not question for one moment the integrity of Professor Denison, or the validity of the experiments which he has conducted for what they are. But his exhalation theory does not fit the facts of this case, since it depends on the existence of an obstruction of blood in the nasal valve. We are satisfied from the evidence of Dr Hill that the only obstruction was in the lower airways. It is now possible to say, that looking at the case as a whole, including the evidence which was before the jury."

152: "The appellant was the last known adult to see the deceased alive, and the first known adult to see her dead."

153: "His clothing was found upon examination to be spattered with blood in a way which was consistent with him being the attacker."

154: "The clothing of others who went to the aid of the deceased was not similarly spattered."

155: "The spattering on his clothing matched precisely the spattering on the leggings of the deceased, which latter spattering was undoubtedly caused by the attacker."

156: "During the initial stages of the police enquiry, the appellant repeatedly failed to reveal that he had been in the house about 15 minutes before the body was discovered, and indeed stated that he had been away for much longer than that."

157: "The appellant's explanation for his absence from the home during the 15 minutes or so immediately prior to the discovery was itself unusual in that he went without money by a circuitous route to buy an item that he did not need."

158: "Although it may be possible for an injured person to exhale a fine spray of blood onto the clothing of someone nearby…"

159: "No one claims to have seen any signs of the deceased breathing."

160: "In order to spatter the appellant with the blood which was found upon him, the deceased would, whilst unconscious and in the prone position, flat on the ground, have had to have her head in such a position that one nostril was about 20 centimetres above the ground, and angled upwards to the extent of 30 to 45 degrees upwards towards the appellant at a time when he was crouched down beside her. At that moment she would then have to have released about 62.5 mls of breath at a pressure of 15mm Hg for 0.1 seconds. The amount of breath released and the period of release might have been greater, but not so great as to render her lungs less than hyper-inflated when her airways became re-obstructed."

161: "Even if all of that were achieved, blood spattering would not, it seems reach the height on the appellant's clothing at which spattering was found."

162: "We conclude that the fresh evidence though relevant and credible, adds so little to the weight of the defence case as compared with the prosecution case, that any doubt induced by the fresh evidence would not be a reasonable doubt. We therefore dismiss the appeal against conviction."

Source: Transcript: R v SION DAVID CHARLES JENKINS: Case No 98/4720 W3 . Royal Courts of Justice, Strand London.

IN THE COURT OF CRIMINAL APPEAL (CRIMINAL DIVISION). Date: 21 December 1999

THE SECOND APPEAL

The Criminal Cases Review Commission (CCRC) investigated the case and heard evidence from a scientific expert witness called by the defence whose conclusions had been rejected by the judges at the first appeal in 1999, Professor David Denison.

This expert witness claimed that the bloodspots could have resulted from a rare condition which would have caused gases to build up in Billie-Jo's lungs, causing her to breathe out blood involuntarily. Having carried out a thorough analysis of the evidence, on 12 May 2003, the CCRC referred the case back for a second appeal.

No. 2003/02883/B4

Neutral Citation Number: [2004] EWCA Crim 2047
IN THE COURT OF APPEAL
CRIMINAL DIVISION

Royal Courts of Justice
The Strand
London
WC2A 2LL

Friday 16 July 2004

Before:

THE VICE PRESIDENT OF THE COURT OF APPEAL CRIMINAL DIVISION
(Lord Justice Rose)

MR JUSTICE CURTIS

and

MR JUSTICE WAKERLEY

REGINA

- v -

SION DAVID CHARLES JENKINS

Computer Aided Transcription by
Smith Bernal, 190 Fleet Street, London EC4
Telephone 020-7421 4040
(Official Shorthand Writers to the Court)

MISS C MONTGOMERY QC and MR J KNOWLES
appeared on behalf of **THE APPELLANT**

MR CAMDEN-PRATT QC and MR A GARDNER
appeared on behalf of **THE CROWN**

JUDGMENT

(As Approved by the Court)

They produced what was known as 'The Statement of Reasons'. The statement, in this case, was powerfully argued and made it very clear that the case had been referred back primarily because of the re-interviewing of the Jenkins' children, Annie and Charlotte.

In the Commission's view, these constituted new evidence. In other words, it was not put before the jury in the original trial, despite it suggesting that Mr Jenkins could not have committed the murder.

The Commission pointed out that the girls were "crucial alibi witnesses". The defence had been unfairly deprived of their evidence at the original trial because of Lois Jenkins' police reports. The Crown Prosecution Service (CPS) had deliberately drawn the material to the attention of the defence. This material had then mistakenly led the defence to believe that the girls had changed their evidence and were now hostile towards Sion Jenkins. However, the Commission asserted that the information in those police records was "inaccurate in important respects".

The new evidence obtained from interviews called into question what had been said by their mother about Annie and Charlotte having changed their account. As a consequence, the defence in reaching its decision not to call the girls at the first trial had been wrong-footed.

A re-interview of Annie and Charlotte was arranged by the CCRC but conducted by an outside police force (Kent Police), and took place on 5 February, 2002. At this re-interview, the CCRC had been impressed by Annie and Charlotte: "Both girls are giving honest responses and are trying their best to say only what they actually remember. Neither girl gives the impression that they are trying to say what they think is required of them. It is clear that they are fully aware of the implications of their answers, not just for their father but also for their mother in that they are being asked to clarify whether what she told the police was in fact accurate and truthful".

The Commission set aside the prosecution's suggestion that Sion may have coached Annie by saying that this was not as certain as previously implied. The CCRC also considered other aspects of the case. At trial, the prosecution case had been based on the presumption that the scientific evidence pointed unquestionably to Sion Jenkins' guilt.

The CCRC now begged to differ.

"The Commission does not consider that the scientific evidence unequivocally establishes that the bloodspots on Mr Jenkins could only be as a result of him being the murderer."

The Commission had also carefully examined the evidence in relation to the other suspect, Mark Lynam. They pointed out that they had access to all the material on the HOLMES database, and were able to perform a much more thorough assessment of all the evidence than the defence had a chance to do.

This analysis led to two important conclusions. Firstly, it was not possible to say with certainty that Lynam was alibied, as the analysis does show some gaps in time. Secondly, it could not be proven that all the clothing he was wearing on the day in question, had in fact been tested for blood.

The CCRC's two-year analysis of all the evidence in the case shows that the jurors at Jenkins' original trial in 1998 had been given disastrously incorrect information. They were told that Mark Lynam, the alternative suspect, could not have committed the crime because he had an alibi, and because his clothing was not bloodstained, which was patently untrue. In all of these important respects, the original trial had been seriously misinformed.

At the second appeal, Lois Jenkins, the then wife of Sion, was accused of distorting the truth and attempting to turn Jenkins' daughters Annie and Charlotte against their father because she (Lois) was convinced that he was the killer. This was claimed on the opening day of the second appeal against conviction.

Sion's counsel, Clare Montgomery QC, told the three appeal judges that fresh evidence gathered since Sion Jenkins was convicted would prove "that Sion Jenkins has not only suffered the tragic loss of a child through murder, but has also been wrongly convicted of that murder".

Among the main pieces of evidence are statements from two of Jenkins' four natural daughters, Charlotte and Annie. They were both with him when he discovered the body of Billie-Jo, which show that their father did not have the time to commit the murder, it was claimed. Both of the girls were never called to give evidence because their mother lied to the police, claiming that one daughter believed her father was the killer, and that both had said he argued with Billie-Jo on the day of the murder.

Charlotte, now 18, had travelled to Britain from her new home in Tasmania, to give evidence in the Court of Appeal. Her sister Annie, made a statement in a video recording which the appeal judges had viewed.

Ms Montgomery recalled what she described as the 'improbable' prosecution case. It was alleged that, during a three-minute visit to the family home on the afternoon of 15 February 1997, Jenkins flew into a rage with Billie-Jo. Then, it was claimed, he battered her more than ten times with a tent-peg, and pushed part of a plastic bin-liner into her nose, before leaving with Charlotte and Annie on a shopping trip.

The far more likely explanation was that Billie-Jo was killed by an intruder who entered through the side gate, it was claimed. Ms Montgomery said the evidence from the two girls made it almost impossible for their father to have been the killer. By their accounts, Billie-Jo was alive when they left the house after the brief visit, and their father came out of the house almost immediately afterwards. He would have had no time to kill her.

Lois Jenkins had told police of conversations she had with Charlotte and Annie in the months following the murder. It was alleged that they made comments which conflicted with their original police statements.

Among the most damaging assertions in the police reports of their conversations were that Jenkins and Billie-Jo had an argument on the day of the murder, and Charlotte "knew" that her father had killed Billie-Jo but not deliberately. Ms Montgomery said interviews with the girls in 2002 showed clearly that the most significant of the statements attributed to them were either not made at all, or not made in the terms in which they were reported by Lois Jenkins. She argued that Lois Jenkins had been faced with a terrible dilemma when, ten days after the killing, she was convinced by the police that her husband was responsible.

Ms Montgomery said: "So, you have a mother who believes her husband, the father of her children, has killed one of them. She is terrified about him returning home and she understands that the children's evidence might lead to her murderous and dangerous husband being released and being sent back into the family. Any mother faced with that prospect, would try and unpick the children's stories".

Another key aspect of the prosecution was evidence from forensic scientists who said that 158 microscopic specks of blood found on Jenkins' clothes, could only have been produced during a frenzied attack on Billie-Jo. Ms Montgomery said that "new evidence would show that the blood spots were more likely to have been caused by blood 'exhaled' across her body".

It was revealed that the former wife of Sion Jenkins wrote to her then-husband as he awaited his first trial, asking him to confess to the killing. The Court of Appeal was told that Lois Jenkins wanted Sion Jenkins to admit to the murder of the 13-year-old for the sake of their other children. The letter was read out as Mrs Jenkins was being cross-examined at the hearing in which her former husband was appealing against his murder conviction and life sentence.

Sion Jenkins' lawyers argued that, as Mrs Jenkins became convinced of her husband's guilt, she fabricated incriminating evidence for fear that her husband would be freed.

The defence counsel, Clare Montgomery, QC, suggested that Mrs Jenkins tried "to convince your husband to confess that he had killed Billie-Jo for the sake of the children so that their daughters Annie and Charlotte who were with him on the day of the murder, would not have to give evidence themselves".

Mrs Jenkins said: "I did not see Sion Jenkins kill Billie-Jo and I will never be 100 per cent sure, but there is a difference between 100 per cent and thinking, and this is a personal letter".

Mrs Jenkins revealed during cross-examination the psychological damage and trauma the murder had caused her daughters. She said that neither of them had properly spoken together about the day of the murder or received any in-depth counselling.

As part of the appeal process, Charlotte, now 18, and Annie 20, agreed to be interviewed again by the police about the murder. Ms Montgomery put it to her that her daughters were a far greater concern to her than her husband, after Billie-Jo's murder.

Mrs Jenkins replied: "I had to make a decision, either to look after my children, or they will fall and crumble..."

In his appeal, Jenkins' legal team alleged that his wife lied to the police and gave the impression that the girls were hostile towards him, and that this deterred his original trial lawyers from calling their potentially crucial evidence on his behalf.

Earlier, the court heard that Mrs Jenkins, a nurse, who now lived with her daughters and her new partner in Tasmania, had told police that her daughter, Annie, had suggested that her husband had killed Billie-Jo because she had upset Annie.

At the second appeal, the judges dismissed the claim that Mr Jenkins was deprived of the chance to call daughters Charlotte and Annie as alibi witnesses because they had turned hostile towards him under the influence of their mother. Also, the judges cleared Mrs Jenkins of the allegation that the two girls had been 'got at' by her to prevent them giving evidence in support of their father.

The third part of the appeal that a mentally-ill man who was close to the murder scene at the time of the attack, was rejected by the judges. They concluded that there was no evidence that the mentally-ill man killed Billie-Jo.

THE FIRST RE-TRIAL

Jurors were told by the judge, Mrs Justice Rafferty at the opening of Jenkins' first re-trial at the Old Bailey on 22 April, 2005, that it was "a completely fresh start", and that they must make up their minds solely on the evidence presented to them.

Sion Jenkins who was facing a re-trial for murder, denied the charge. The court was told that Billie-Jo spent the morning of her death at the Jenkins' family home where she lived with her foster parents and four sisters. The teenager had been painting a door and may have made a mess, causing Mr Jenkins to lose his temper, the jury was told by prosecuting counsel Nicholas Hilliard QC.

An 18-inch tent peg was used to beat the girl over the head at least five times. There was evidence that Jenkins, the former teacher, had previously lost his temper and used violence against Billie-Jo. It was also claimed that Mr Jenkins was also under considerable stress because he had lied on his CV (he fabricated and exaggerated his academic qualifications to get a new job as a headteacher).

The court was told that, on the day before the murder, Mr Jenkins and his wife went out for a drink and argued about Billie-Jo. Counsel for the prosecution said that Mr Jenkins lied to the police about his whereabouts at the time of the murder, only telling officers three days later that he was inside the house. Mr Hilliard said: "The defendant was the last adult to see Billie-Jo alive and the first adult to find her body". There was no sign that Billie-Jo had been sexually assaulted and nothing was stolen.

Mr Jenkins said that he left the house with two of his daughters to go to a DIY store, and Billie-Jo must have been killed after that point. When they returned, he went inside and found Billie-Jo's body. This first retrial ended with the jury failing to reach a verdict, and a further re-trial of Sion Jenkins was ordered by the judge.

This first new murder trial centred on the interpretation of the new forensic material. Forensic scientists stated that the microscopic bloodspots could conceivably have been released from Billie-Jo's injured airway as Sion Jenkins attempted to move her. After 30 hours of deliberation, the jury was unable to reach a majority verdict.

THE SECOND RE-TRIAL

This trial began on 31 October, 2005. It looked set to be brought on the basis that guilt could be proved not by the invisible bloodspots themselves, not by the 'white inclusions' at the centre of some of these spots, but even more 'microscopic fragments' within the 'white inclusions' within the 'invisible spots'.

As it turned out, fragments of human material whether bone, brain matter or anything else, were not present in these 'invisible spots". Nicholas Hilliard, QC, the prosecuting counsel, said it was the crown's case that

Mr Jenkins was the killer of Billie-Jo.

He said:

"She had been murdered at her own home, a place where she should have been safe. She had been struck at least five times and sustained severe head injuries. It does not take a moment to hit someone with an iron bar, and not many more to hit them several forceful blows. If she did not die instantly, she could not have lived more than a few minutes. It's a mercy she was unconscious."

Mr Hilliard said the iron tent peg had been placed in the patio earlier in the day by one of the other children whilst she was clearing out a utility room. This had been found near Billie-Jo's body after she was discovered by Mr Jenkins and two of his daughters when they returned from a DIY store. Mr Hilliard said that Mr Jenkins was the last adult to see Billie-Jo alive and the first adult to find her body. The jury were told that traces of Billie-Jo's blood were found on Mr Jenkins' clothing. They would have to consider whether it got there when she was attacked or after he discovered the body.

Mr Hilliard said that Mr Jenkins had failed at first to tell police he had been inside the house that afternoon before going to the DIY store. Mr Jenkins later said he had gone into the dining room to turn down Billie-Jo's music, but had not noticed her on the other side of the patio doors.

"How did he come to give the earlier different version to the police? Had he just forgotten or was he lying about it?" asked Mr Hilliard. Mr Jenkins had said that, as far as he was aware, Billie-Jo was alive and well when he left the house to buy some white spirits. The court was told that he had claimed someone else must have come to the house and murdered Billie-Jo the court was told.

At midday on Thursday 9 February, 2006, Sion Jenkins stepped out of Court Seven at the Old Bailey, knowing that the jury's failure to reach a verdict meant that the worst of his nine-year ordeal was now over.

Despite hours of deliberations, the jury of six women and six men were, once again, unable to agree which version of the story was the correct one. Following the hung jury, the judge, Mr Justice Clarke said he would accept a 10-2 majority. Nicholas Hilliard for the prosecution said no further retrial would be sought. He remarked:

"In the course of two lengthy trials, neither jury has been able to reach a verdict, and we can't say they would be more likely than not to do so in a future trial".

Mr Justice Clarke recorded a formal 'Not Guilty' verdict.

In the eyes of the law, Sion Jenkins was an innocent man. The Crown Prosecution Service decided to acquit Mr Jenkins because they did believe that there was enough evidence to provide a 'realistic prospect of conviction' or that a prosecution was 'not in the public interest'.

Part of the reason not to have a fourth trial, was that the majority of two juries were not convinced by the forensic evidence, and Crown prosecutors would have trouble in getting Lois Jenkins to give evidence for a fourth time.

Only a handful of cases have ever been tried three times, and only one is believed to have gone to a fourth trial. This was the case of *R v Henworth (1996)*. For the natural family of the dead girl, and for Mr Jenkins' former wife, the matter remains far from over. Many will be disturbed to learn of evidence in Mr Jenkins' appeal not made public at the time, or of accusations that the former teacher had a long history of domestic abuse and an explosive temper, as alleged by Mrs Jenkins.

To date, the crime remains unsolved.

CHAPTER SIX

MEDIA RESPONSES

"On Monday 12 May, 2003, Sion Jenkins had his case referred to the Court of Appeal to consider evidence not used in the original trial. Jenkins was jailed for life for bludgeoning to death 13-year-old Billie-Jo Jenkins, with an 18-inch metal tent peg as she painted a patio door at their home in Hastings, East Sussex in 1997. The jury at the First Trial held at Lewes Crown Court in 1998, was told after the killing, Jenkins went shopping with two of his four daughters, and later pretended to discover Billie-Jo's body when he returned. There were more than 150 microscopic spots of the teenager's blood discovered on Jenkins' jacket which were consistent only with his having been the attacker, the court heard.

At the Court of Appeal in December 1999, Jenkins' barrister Anthony Scrivener QC, claimed the former deputy headteacher's jacket had been contaminated with the blood as he attended the dying girl because a bubble of blood burst in her nose and it splashed him. Jenkins lost the appeal, and in January 2000, was refused leave to appeal to the House of Lords. But in April 2001, a file containing new evidence was handed to the Criminal Cases Review Commission (CCRC). The Commission had decided that there was a 'real possibility' Jenkins' conviction would be quashed by the Court of Appeal. According to Jenkins' solicitors, the appeal related to why Jenkins' two daughters were not called at the trial to give evidence. "It is pretty important to hear from the two people who were with Sion Jenkins throughout the afternoon when Billie-Jo died" said

Neil O'May, partner at the London solicitors, Bindman and Partners.

Jenkins' legal team will also pursue the suggestion by Channel 4's *Trial and Error* programme which investigates alleged miscarriages of justice, that a mentally-ill man seen near the family home in Hastings, could have been the killer. The appeal hearing will also consider the evidence of the pathologist.

Mr O' May said: "The CCRC has thoroughly investigated the case and believes there is a real possibility that Sion Jenkins' conviction will be quashed. We have investigated the circumstances of the conviction very thoroughly, and we are confident the Court of Appeal will mark the case as a miscarriage of justice".

The CCRC is an independent body with the power to re-open cases if it suspects a miscarriage of justice, and refer them to the Court of Appeal."

Source: The Independent, 13, May,2003. Author: Robert Verkauk, Legal Affairs Correspondent.

"INQUIRY TO BE HELD INTO NEW EVIDENCE IN BILLIE-JO CASE"

"An investigation has been ordered into new evidence that could help clear Sion Jenkins, the former deputy headteacher convicted of murdering his foster daughter, Billie-Jo in 1997. The Court of Appeal ordered yesterday that evidence about the behaviour of a mentally-ill man who was near the murder scene and who was considered a suspect, must be re-examined. Jenkins' trial in 1998 heard that the man who was known to have been in the vicinity when Billie-Jo Jenkins, 13, was killed at her home in Hastings, East Sussex, may have had a fixation with pushing pieces of plastic bags up his nose. Three appeal judges in London were told yesterday that a pathologist found Billie-Jo had part of a black bin-liner stuffed deeply into one of her nostrils after her murder. The man, a paranoid schizophrenic, had been seen in a park near the murder scene.

The appeal judges have asked the Criminal Cases Review Commission to inquire into whether the man exhibited any unusual behaviour in relation to plastic bags or sheets or other plastic objects. Clare Montgomery QC, who is representing Jenkins, told the appeal court judges at a preliminary hearing yesterday, that the plastic found in the girl's nose was "a singular and striking feature of the murder". Jenkins, 46, was jailed for life for bludgeoning Billie-Jo to death with a metal tent-peg, as she painted a patio door at their home."

Source: The Independent, 5, March, 2004. Author: Jason Bennetto.

"CONVICTED OF MURDERING HIS FOSTER DAUGHTER BUT WILL NEW EVIDENCE CLEAR SION JENKINS?"

"The Victorian house on Lower Park Road in the East Sussex seaside town of Hastings, has recently undergone a transformation. Both front and back gardens have been given a smart makeover. Some 250 miles away in a cell in Wakefield high security prison in West Yorkshire, lives the former owner, Sion Jenkins. He too is hoping for a fresh start. It was at the back garden of the semi-detached property in February 1997, that a crime was committed which caused national revulsion, and led to Jenkins becoming one of the country's most vilified figures. The deputy headteacher was convicted in July 1998 of bludgeoning his 13-year-old foster daughter, Billie-Jo, with a metal tent peg in a fit of rage. He was sentenced to life for the murder.

Nearly six years after the trial, startling new evidence is beginning to emerge which raises disturbing questions about Jenkins guilt, and which could lead to his acquittal later this year. The Court of Appeal has ordered a new investigation into the actions of a mentally-ill man who was the police's first suspect for the murder. Lawyers for Jenkins have also obtained expert forensic analysis which challenges the prosecution's key evidence about bloodstains found on the teacher. The third plank of the Court of Appeal challenge by Jenkins' legal team is two of his daughters who the defence claim can provide their father with an alibi. They will be crossed-examined and will give live evidence for the first time at the Appeal hearing later this year.

The Criminal Cases Review Commission (CCRC) which investigates suspected miscarriages of justice, referred the case to the Court of Appeal last year, after re-examining the evidence given at the original trial, and the fresh evidence produced by the defence. Nevertheless, the police are adamant that they got the right man, and the Crown Prosecution Service will be defending the conviction in court. If Jenkins were to be freed at the hearing which is expected to take place in summer, it will be hugely controversial and lead to the obvious question, if he did not murder Billie-Jo, then who did?

The brutality and apparent randomness of a crime committed by a churchgoer and a respected member of the community shocked the nation. At his trial in Lewes Crown Court, the jury heard that Billie-Jo's body was discovered on the patio at the back of the family home where she lived with her foster family, Sion, his wife Lois, a social worker, and their four daughters. The prosecution successfully argued that Jenkins, now 46, had returned to the house in the afternoon of Saturday 15 February 1997, with two of his daughters, Annie and Charlotte. He entered the house where Billie-Jo had been painting the patio doors, and in an uncontrollable rage, bludgeoned her to death. He then took his two daughters out to a DIY store in order to create a false alibi for himself. On their return to the house, he found the body and called 999 for help. The prosecution was unable to suggest any reason why Jenkins might have committed the murder. After his conviction, it emerged that he had struck out at his wife on a number of occasions, and had once kicked his stepdaughter. The police suggested that he simply lost his temper, possibly provoked by Billie-Jo playing loud music. The crucial forensic evidence against Jenkins at his trial was the discovery of 158 microscopic bloodspots on his clothing. A forensic scientist successfully argued that the thin mist of droplets was created as Jenkins swung the 18-inch tent-peg, striking his foster daughter at least nine times.

Jenkins' legal team challenged the forensic evidence in an appeal in 1999, but the court rejected the challenge. Since then, fresh evidence has emerged following inquiries by the defence team headed by the lawyer Neil O'May, and investigators from the CCRC. One of the principal issues surrounds a paranoid schizophrenic man who had been seen sitting in a park within eight minutes' walk of the murder scene at the time of Billie-Jo's death. The man who cannot be named for legal reasons, was arrested by the police after a guest-house owner living in Jenkins' road, reported that he had been behaving strangely on the night of the murder. He was later eliminated from the inquiry after Sussex Police found at least three witnesses who said he was in the park at the time of the murder. It has since emerged that when the man was arrested and placed in cells, he tried to stuff into his mouth a piece of plastic that he had been keeping hidden in his clothing. It was later confiscated by police. This is considered potentially significant because part of a plastic bin-liner was found buried deeply in Billie-Jo's left nostril.

The CCRC has now been asked to investigate whether the man had a fixation with plastic bags. The man who resisted arrest, was never questioned because he was considered medically unfit. Items of his clothing were forensically tested but no bloodstains were discovered. But the defence believes that he may have destroyed some clothing. There are also questions being asked about the accuracy of the timings given by witnesses, who saw him in the park. There is also a dispute over the evidence given by Jenkins' daughters, Annie and Charlotte, now aged 19 and 17 respectively. Neither the police nor the defence called the girls to give evidence at the trial, instead, relying on a police video interview which was interpreted as giving Jenkins 'a few minutes' opportunity to murder Billie-Jo.

The CCRC re-interviewed the girls in 2002, and the defence now believes that the original defence team were 'wrong footed' or misled at the trial, and that the teenagers' testimony provides their father with an alibi for the time of the murder. Annie and Charlotte will be cross-examined at the Court of Appeal in the summer, and it will be up to the judges to decide whether their evidence is admissible. The third area of dispute is over the forensic evidence. In the Appeal Court, two professors from Sheffield University will argue that evidence given at the original trial was wrong. These forensic specialists will say that air trapped in Billie-Jo's dead body, possibly by a blood clot, could have been released by her foster father as he attended her, and thus have produced the thin mist of blood droplets. They will also question why Jenkins did not have more blood on him considering the huge amounts of fluid lost during the savage attack.

Throughout his campaign to prove his innocence, Jenkins has maintained the support of his parents, David and Megan, and a small group of supporters. But his relationship with his wife Lois, has deteriorated. Soon after Jenkins' conviction, she remarried and moved her family to Australia. She has also written a newspaper article complaining about the 'self-righteous justice industry'. Despite the new appeal, the man who helped put Jenkins behind bars, Chief Superintendent Jeremy Paine, the detective who led the inquiry, is unimpressed. He said yesterday: "I would not have charged him with murder unless I was utterly convinced he was guilty of this crime. I remain convinced of it".

Source: The Independent, 6, March, 2004. Author: Jason Bennetto, Crime Correspondent.

"WIFE 'DISTORTED TRUTH' OVER BILLIE-JO MURDER"

"The wife of Sion Jenkins, the schoolteacher convicted of murdering his foster-daughter, Billie-Jo, lied about crucial evidence that could have helped clear her husband, the Court of Appeal was told yesterday. Lois Jenkins was accused of "distorting the truth" and attempting to turn Jenkins' daughters, Charlotte and Annie', against their father because she was convinced that he was a killer, it was claimed on the opening day of an appeal against the conviction. Jenkins was jailed for life at Lewes Crown Court for bludgeoning 13-year-old Billie-Jo to death with an 18-inch metal tent peg as she painted a patio door at their home in Hastings, East Sussex in February, 1997. Fresh evidence gathered since Jenkins was convicted would prove "that Sion Jenkins has not only suffered the tragic loss of a child through murder, but has also been wrongly convicted of that murder", his counsel Clare Montgomery QC, told three appeal judges.

Among the main pieces of evidence are Statements from two of Jenkins' four natural daughters, Charlotte and Annie, who were with him when he discovered the body, which show that their father did not have time to commit the murder, it was claimed in court. But the girls were never called to give evidence because their mother lied to the police, claiming one daughter believed her father was the killer, and that both had said he argued with Billie-Jo on the day of the murder, the court was told. Charlotte, now 18 has travelled to Britain from her new home in Tasmania to give evidence in the Court of Appeal, and her sister Annie 20, has made a statement in a video recording seen by the judges. Their mother, Lois, who divorced Jenkins soon after his conviction, and moved to Australia with a new partner, is to give evidence for the Crown in its opposition to his fresh appeal.

Ms Montgomery recalled what she described as the 'inappropriate' prosecution case. It was alleged that, during a three-minute visit to the family home on the afternoon of 15 February 1997, Jenkins flew into a rage with Billie-Jo. Then, it was claimed he battered her more than ten times with a tent peg and pushed part of a plastic bin liner into her nose before leaving with Charlotte and Annie on a shopping trip. The far more likely explanation was that Billie-Jo was killed by an intruder who entered through the side gate, it was claimed. Ms Montgomery said the evidence from the two girls made it almost impossible for their father to have been the murderer. On their accounts, Billie-Jo was alive when they left the house after the brief visit and their father came out almost immediately afterwards. He would have had no time to kill her. Lois Jenkins had told police of conversations she had with the two girls in the months following the murder in which they allegedly made comments conflicting with their original accounts.

Among the most damaging assertions in the police reports of these communications, were that Jenkins and Billie-Jo had an argument on the day of the murder and that Charlotte 'knew' that her father had killed Billie-Jo but believed he had not done it deliberately. Ms Montgomery said interviews with the girls in 2002 showed that the most significant of the statements attributed to them were either not made at all, or not made in the terms in which they were reported. She argued that Lois Jenkins had been faced with a 'terrible dilemma' when ten days after the killing, she was convinced by the police that her husband was responsible.

Ms Montgomery said:

"So you have a mother who believes her husband, the father of her children, has killed one of them She is terrified about him returning home and she understands that the children's evidence nevertheless, might lead to her murderous and dangerous husband being released and being sent back into the family. Any mother faced with that prospect will try and unpick the children's stories."

Another key aspect of the prosecution, was evidence from forensic scientists who said that 150 microscopic specks of blood found on Jenkins' clothes could only have been produced during a frenzied attack on Billie-Jo. Ms Montgomery said new evidence would show that the blood spots were more likely to have been caused by blood exhaled from the girl's airways as he leant across her."

Source: The Independent, 1 July, 2004. Author: Jason Bennetto - Crime Correspondent.

"EX- WIFE OF JENKINS ASKED HIM TO ADMIT TO BILLIE-JO MURDER"

"The former wife of the teacher convicted of murdering his foster daughter, Billie-Jo Jenkins, wrote to her husband as he awaited trial asking him to confess to the killing, it was revealed yesterday. Lois Jenkins wanted Sion Jenkins to admit to the murder of the 13-year-old for the sake of their other children, the Court of Appeal was told. In a letter written to Jenkins on 13 April, 1997, while he was on bail, she wrote:

"The girls would, I know, be relieved of enormous burdens if they felt human beings had the capacity to own up to things. I am living in constant awareness of the need

for the children and others to experience again the reality of honesty and confession".

The letter was read out as Mrs Jenkins was being cross-examined at the hearing in which her former husband is appealing against his murder conviction and life sentence. Jenkins' lawyers argued that as Mrs Jenkins became convinced of her husband's guilt, she fabricated incriminating evidence for fear that her husband would be freed.

Clare Montgomery, QC for the defence, suggested that Mrs Jenkins tried to convince her husband to confess that he had killed Billie-Jo for the sake of the children "so that their daughters Annie and Charlotte who were with him on the day of the murder, would not have to give evidence".

Mrs Jenkins said:

"I did not see Sion Jenkins kill Billie-Jo and I will never be 100 per cent sure, but there is a difference between 100 per cent and thinking, and this is a personal letter".

Mrs Jenkins revealed during cross-examination, the psychological damage and trauma the murder caused her daughters. She said neither of them had properly spoken together about the day of the murder or received any in-depth counselling.

As part of the appeal process, Charlotte now 18, and Annie 20, agreed to be interviewed again by the police about the murder. Ms Montgomery put it to her that her daughters were a far greater concern to her than her husband after Billie-Jo's death.

Mrs Jenkins replied: "I had to make a decision, either I look after my children or they will fall and crumble".

In this appeal, Jenkins' legal team alleges that his wife lied to the police and gave the impression that the girls were hostile towards him, and that this deterred his trial lawyers from calling their potentially crucial evidence on his behalf. Earlier, the court heard that Mrs Jenkins, a nurse who now lives with her daughters and her new partner in Tasmania, had told police that her daughter Annie 'had suggested that her husband had killed Billie-Jo because she had upset Annie'".

Source: The Independent, 7, July, 2004. Author: Jason Bennetto, Crime Correspondent.

"JENKINS WINS RE-TRIAL OVER MURDER OF FOSTER DAUGHTER"

"Sion Jenkins will stand trial again for the murder of his foster daughter after the Court of Appeal yesterday, quashed his conviction. New scientific evidence convinced the appeal judges in London that the conviction in 1998 for the killing of Billie-Jo was unsafe. Mr Jenkins showed no emotion as he was told he was no longer considered guilty of one of the most notorious killings of the 1990s. The new trial is expected at the Old Bailey within a year. Mr Jenkins' solicitor Neil O'May said after the ruling:

"He knows this is the first step to clear his name and he knows a jury will deliver the right verdict that he did not kill Billie-Jo".

A decision has yet to be made on whether 46-year-old Mr Jenkins will be given bail, of if he has to remain in prison until the trial. He has already served six years after having been convicted of battering 13-year-old Billie-Jo to death with a metal tent-peg. The case pitted Mr Jenkins against his wife Lois, 43, who has since divorced him and who gave evidence for the Crown against her former husband during his appeal hearing. Lord Justice Rose sitting with Mr Justice Curtis and Mr Justice Wakerley, quashed the conviction on the basis of new forensic evidence. This was disclosed by Mr Jenkins' defence only four days before the appeal began, and provided for the first time a different explanation of how tiny droplets of Billie-Jo's blood could have been sprayed on his trousers and jacket.

The spatter on Mr Jenkins was the 'crux of the case' against him, Lord Justice Rose said in his judgment. This was the second appeal hearing for Mr Jenkins, and follows an investigation by the Criminal Cases Review Commission, the body that examines alleged miscarriages of justice. At Mr Jenkins' trial at Lewes Crown Court, the jury was told that, during a three-minute visit to the family home, he had an argument with Billie-Jo and hit her over the head up to ten times. He is then said to have driven off with two of his four natural daughters, Charlotte and Annie, who were aged 10 and 12 at the time. The case against him was founded on evidence of more than 150 microscopic spots of Billie-Jo's blood on his clothing. The prosecution said they were 'impact spatter' caused as Mr Jenkins beat the girl to death. Mr Jenkins' defence countered this at his appeal that droplets of blood were forced out of Billie-Jo's lungs as he moved her body in an attempt to help her.

The appeal judge said this was a credible theory because new scientific evidence showed that at some time after the attack, Billie-Jo's upper airway was blocked and that pressure in her lungs built up behind the blockage. The evidence emerged after a pathologist examined tiny sections of the dead girl's lungs that had been kept on slides. The judge said that if the original trial jury had had the opportunity to hear the evidence, the verdict might have been different. The new murder trial is likely to centre on the interpretation of this fresh material. Earlier the judges dismissed a claim made in the appeal hearing that Mr Jenkins was deprived of the chance to call Charlotte and Annie as alibi witnesses, because they had turned hostile towards him under the influence of their mother.

The judges cleared Mrs Jenkins of the allegation that the girls had been 'got at' by her to stop them giving evidence in support of their father. The former Mrs Jenkins and her daughters may refuse to give evidence at the new trial, in which case the defence and prosecution will have to rely on video testimonies already made. A third plank of the appeal that a mentally-ill man who was close to the murder scene at the time of the crime could have been responsible, was also rejected by the judges. They concluded that there was no evidence that the man killed Billie-Jo. Outside court, Chief Superintendent Jeremy Paine from Sussex Police, said: "The Court has made its decision, and we will get ready for a re-trial".

Source: The Independent, 17 July, 2004. Author: Jason Bennetto -Crime Correspondent.

"BILLIE-JO'S FOSTER FATHER ACCUSED OF PAST ATTACK"

"Sion Jenkins, the former deputy headteacher accused of battering his foster-daughter, Billie-Jo, to death, had previously attacked the 13-year-old while on holiday, the Old Bailey was told yesterday. Mr Jenkins, 47, allegedly used a large iron tent peg to kill the girl at the family home in Hastings, East Sussex in February, 1997. He is facing a re-trial for murder. Jurors were told by the judge, Mrs Justice Rafferty, at the Old Bailey yesterday, that it was a "completely fresh start" and they must make up their minds solely on the evidence presented to them. Mr Jenkins denies murder. The court was told on the opening day of the trial that Billie-Jo spent the morning of her death at the Jenkins' family home where she lived with her foster parents and four sisters. The teenager had been painting a door and may have made a mess, causing Mr Jenkins to lose his temper, the jury was told.

An 18-inch tent-peg was used to beat the girl over the head at least five times. There was evidence that the former teacher had previously lost his temper and used violence against Billie-Jo. It was claimed Mr Jenkins was also under 'considerable strain' because he had lied on his CV which he fabricated and exaggerated his qualifications to get a new job as a headteacher. The previous alleged assault happened in August, 1996, when the family were on holiday with friends when Billie-Jo twisted her ankle. Peter Gaimster, who was on holiday with the Jenkins, reported hearing Billie-Jo crying and went to investigate. Nicholas Hilliard QC, for the prosecution said: "He went upstairs and saw the defendant kick Billie-Jo with full force on her injured leg. It is a particularly cruel thing to do, particularly to a child. Mr Jenkins is a big man".

The court heard that Billie-Jo moved in with the Jenkins in 1992 when they lived in East London. Shortly afterwards they moved to Hastings. The court was told that on the day before the murder, Mr Jenkins and his wife Lois went out for a drink and argued about Billie-Jo. Mr Hilliard said Mr Jenkins lied to police about his whereabouts at the time of the murder, only telling officers three days later, that he was inside the house. "The defendant was the last adult to see Billie-Jo alive and the first adult to find her body", Mr Hillard said. There was no sign that Billie-Jo was sexually assaulted and nothing was stolen. Mr Jenkins said he left the house with two of his daughters to go to a DIY store, and Billie-Jo must have been killed after that point. When they returned, he went inside and found Billie-Jo's body. The prosecution did not accept he had tried to do everything to care for her after finding her. When the ambulance arrived, he told police he went inside. But before he showed them where to go, he said, he got into his sports car to put up the roof."

Source: The Independent, 21, April, 2005. Author: Jason Bennetto, Crime Correspondent.

"BILLIE-JO JENKINS DIED MINUTES AFTER ATTACK, COURT TOLD"

"Billie-Jo Jenkins was battered around the head five times with an iron bar and died within minutes, an Old Bailey jury was told. Sion Jenkins, a former deputy headteacher went on trial yesterday, for the second time this year, accused of murdering his 13-year-old foster daughter. Mr Jenkins denies killing Billie-Jo. In 1998, Mr Jenkins was convicted and jailed for life, but was released on bail last year. During a retrial which ended in July, the jury failed to reach a verdict. The six men and six women on the new jury, were told by the judge that it was a 'completely new trial'.

Nicholas Hilliard QC prosecuting said it was the Crown's case that Mr Jenkins was the killer.

He said:

"She had been murdered at her own home, a place where she should have been safe. She had been attacked with an iron bar. She had been struck at least five times, and sustained severe head injuries. It does not take a moment to hit someone with an iron bar, and not many more to hit them several forceful blows. If she did not die instantly, she could not have lived more than a few minutes. It's a mercy she was unconscious".

Mr Hilliard said the iron tent-peg had been placed in the patio earlier in the day by one of the other children, whilst she was clearing out a utility room. It had been found near Billie-Jo's body after she was discovered by Mr Jenkins and two of his daughters when they returned from the DIY store.

Mr Hilliard said Mr Jenkins was the last adult to see Billie-Jo alive and the first adult to find her body. The jury were told traces of Billie-Jo's blood were found on Mr Jenkins' clothing. They would have to consider whether it got there when she was attacked, or after he discovered the body. He said Mr Jenkins had failed at first to tell police he had been inside the house that afternoon before going to the DIY store. Mr Jenkins later said he had gone into the dining room to turn down Billie-Jo's music but had not noticed her on the other side of the patio doors.

"How did he come to give the earlier different version to police? Had he just forgotten or was he lying about it?"

asked Mr Hilliard.

Mr Jenkins had said that as far as he was aware, Billie-Jo was alive and well when he left the house to buy some white spirit. He had claimed someone else must have come to the house and murdered Billie-Jo, the court was told."

Source: The Independent, 2, November, 2005. Author: Genevieve Roberts.

"NINE-YEAR ORDEAL ENDS AS JURY AQUITS SION JENKINS"

"Just after midday on Tuesday 9 February, 2006, Sion Jenkins stepped out of Court Seven at the Old Bailey, London, knowing that a jury's failure to reach a verdict meant that the worst of his nine-year ordeal was over. He is, in the eyes of the law, an innocent man. His supporters believe his conviction at the first of three trials, to be one of the worst miscarriages of justice in recent times. However, for the natural family of the dead girl, and for Mr Jenkins' former wife, the matter remains far from over. Many will also be disturbed to learn of evidence given at Mr Jenkins' appeal, but not made public at the time, of accusations that the former teacher had a long history of domestic abuse and an explosive temper.

Three times a jury has been asked to decide whether Mr Jenkins was a lying, arrogant bully, responsible for an inexplicable act of violence against his young foster daughter. Each time the jurors had been offered an alternative image; a caring father whose life was ruined by flawed forensic evidence, a vindictive wife and sheer bad luck. Despite 39 hours of deliberations, this time the jury of six women and six men were unable to agree which version of the story was the correct one. After the decision, the Crown Prosecution Service announced that it would not seek a further trial. Mr Jenkins was immediately acquitted by the judge. His ordeal appeared to be over.

As he left the Old Bailey with his new wife, Mr Jenkins said:

"It has taken more than nine years of struggle and faith for me to be standing here today. It has been a terrible ordeal and I find it difficult to actually take it in. Of course, my thoughts today, as always, are with my daughters Annie, Charlotte, Esther and Maya. I want to assure them of my total love for them. Although they are on the other side of the world, not a day has passed without me thinking of them all".

Source: The Independent, 10, February, 2006. Author: Jason Bennetto – Crime Correspondent.

"SION JENKINS HIT BY FRESH CLAIMS ABOUT HIS CHARACTER"

"Her story is one that was never put before jurors in the trial of Sion Jenkins, the former deputy headmaster accused of bludgeoning his foster daughter, Billi-Jo to death with a tent peg. But now, Lois Jenkins has broken her silence to give a devastating account of her life with her 48-year-old ex-husband, who walked free from the Old Bailey last week after his second re-trial collapsed. In an interview with a national newspaper, the mother of four alleges that Jenkins was a liar with a controlling nature who began physically beating her in the first year of their marriage, and used a stick to inflict corporal punishment and had frequent mood swings.

Thirteen-year-old Billie-Jo had been living with the Jenkins family for five years when she was found dead at the family home in Hastings, East Sussex in 1997. Sion Jenkins became the main suspect, and a month later he was charged with murder. In 1998, he was given a life sentence after being found guilty at Lewes Crown Court, but six years later, his conviction was quashed by the Court of Appeal.

A re-trial followed but jurors failed to reach a verdict, which happened again last week. Now living in Tasmania, Mrs Jenkins recalls in her account of their marriage published in *The Mail on Sunday,* that her testimony was ruled inadmissible in court along with her claims that he had a sexual encounter with a teenage girl who bore a strong resemblance to Billie-Jo. Just four days after her foster child was found dead, Mrs Jenkins says she began to suspect her husband might have carried out the savage killing.

"I can recall with clarity the look in his eyes as he told the children 'Billie's Dead'. It had no trace of emotion" she said.

"I woke up in the middle of the night as he turned over in bed, and it dawned on me it could have been him. I lay there terrified, thinking it must be him, and if it wasn't him, at least it could have been him."

In a 7,000-word account, Mrs Jenkins who now lives with a martial arts expert, who is the father of her baby, says that the murder of Billie-Jo 'destroyed' her self confidence in the legal system, and was also the reason that she left England. In the days after Billie-Jo's death, she says it was as though her former husband

"wasn't there. He offered no comfort. I felt let down and also faintly embarrassed. I wondered if our friends had noticed his detachment"

she writes. To outsiders, the Jenkins family appeared

to have the perfect life. Their home was in one of the most attractive parts of Hastings, on the side of an old sandstone gorge, along which sprawls the splendidly renovated Victorian park. The castle and the coloured terraces of the old town can be seen in the distance, and the sea is only a mile away.

But house prices remain relatively low; a six-bedroom property a few doors down is on the market for £275,000. Billie-Jo had an apparently comfortable life with Sion and Lois Jenkins and their four daughters, having been put up for fostering because her natural father was in prison and her mother could not cope. In what she describes as her 'tribute' to her dead foster-daughter, Mrs Jenkins describes Billie-Jo as having a sense of fun and warmth.

"I grew to love her and regard her as my own daughter. She had a good rapport with Sion, and I truly believe she was happy with her new family".

Mrs Jenkins had a good job as the deputy headmaster of William Parker School in Hastings. But after a few years he started hankering after becoming a headmaster in London, and also decided that he wanted to become a politician, even joining the Conservative Party despite his left-wing leanings. It was at this point that Mrs Jenkins says he began to lie about himself and that this created tensions and rows within the marriage.

"He wrote a small manifesto about himself which I knew to be inaccurate. He said that he was a regular theatre-goer, yet we hadn't been to a theatre performance for six years. We argued endlessly about his strange behaviour. These were not the only lies he told. Police discovered that he had lied on his CV claiming to have been educated at the public school Gordonstoun, to secure his job at William Parker School. He had also exaggerated his academic qualifications, and was afraid of getting found out. At home, he had a violent temper which led to angry outbursts if he felt that his control was being

challenged".

Mrs Jenkins says that she never believed that his behaviour was 'normal'.

"I think he felt insecure. I never thought his behaviour was normal but I got used to it. I ended up feeling sorry for him as I felt he was a victim of emotions that he couldn't control".

What worried her more was him punishing their children with a stick after attending a series of talks on the disciplining of children by a man called James Dobson, which was popular in the church that they had attended in London".

Source: The Independent on Sunday, 12 February 2006. Authors: Cole Moreton and Sophie Goodchild.

"IT WAS A SCENE NO ONE SHOULD SEE: I COULD NOT COPE"

"Sion Jenkins, acquitted last month of murdering his 13-year-old foster daughter Billie-Jo, last night spoke in detail for the first time about events surrounding her death. He lashed out at Sussex Police who investigated the crime accusing them of 'using' and 'manipulating' his former wife, Lois, and turning her against him in the original trial eight years ago. In an emotionally charged interview, Mr Jenkins denied claims by Lois that he had been violent during their marriage. He last night described himself as a 'good husband' and 'loving father' who had never beaten his wife. He says that Lois was 'confused' and 'vulnerable' in the wake of the murder, and that the Sussex Police should apologise to her.

"In all the allegations that Lois has put with regard to that I was a wife-beater, this is not true", he says.

Talking to Sir Trevor McDonald for a special edition of ITV's *Tonight* programme which was broadcast on Monday 20 March, 2006, Mr Jenkins claims that his movements and behaviour on the day of the murder were 'presented in a false light' and 'twisted'. The prosecution argued that a fine spray of blood on Mr Jenkins' clothes was caused when he repeatedly struck her with a metal tent peg.

However, at the 2004 Appeal, government scientists conceded that they had 'ignored' post-mortem tests that might have revealed that Billie-Jo suffered from a medical condition that meant air could have been forced into her lower lungs, and caused a mist of blood particles to spray from her nose and mouth when Mr Jenkins was holding her. In court, it was revealed that he had once lied on a CV to get a better teaching job, placing his character, and the value of his testimony in question.

"Maybe 97 per cent of the first trial was fought on science" he tells Sir Trevor.

"Both my appeals were effectively fought on science. My appeal was allowed because of the scientific case that supports my innocence. Suddenly, it was more like 60 per cent science and the other 40 per cent was bad character. You have lied on your CV, that probably means he is guilty."

Mr Jenkins lied on his CV

"because I wanted a better job, to be sure of getting an interview, and so I stupidly exaggerated my qualifications and experience, and after a few years it became an albatross around my neck and I regret it".

Of the moment he found Billie-Jo's blood-spattered body, he says:

"I could not take it in. My world just fell apart. I had my two other daughters with me, Anne and Lotte, and they were crying and were hysterical. I needed to be with Billie-Jo and help her. I had my other children to look after. I had no idea what was happening. There was nobody else to help me. I phoned a friend of the family who only lived a minute away to come over. But it was, it is a scene that no

person should ever see and I couldn't cope with it at all".

Source: The Independent on Sunday, 19 March 2006. Author: Robin Stummer.

"SION JENKINS, FOSTER FATHER OF BILLIE-JO JENKINS LOSES CLAIM FOR COMPENSATION"

"Sion Jenkins, who served six years in jail after being convicted of murdering his foster-daughter, Billie-Jo, before being acquitted, has been refused compensation for his time in prison, according to reports. The former deputy headteacher had sought up to £500,000 in damages for the prison term he served, but the Ministry of Justice has rejected his request after his case was assessed. Jenkins believed he fitted the criteria for a payout, but compensation rules state that applicants for miscarriage of justice compensation must demonstrate that they are 'clearly innocent'. Jenkins, who was found guilty in 1998 of killing 13-year-old Billie-Jo, has always protested his innocence, but his repeated calls for compensation have been rejected.

After his acquittal in February 2006, and following the publication of his book: *'The Murder of Billie-Jo'*, Jenkins said:

"I believe the government should compensate me for taking away my liberty for six years, which also meant I lost the childhood of my daughters. Family members have died while I was inside. I had a lot of kicking. I have raged inside because I have not been able to cope. I believe the government should pay for that. I fulfil all the criteria. The amount is not the important thing".

Source: The Guardian Online, 10 August 2010. Author: Alexandra Topping.

"SION JENKINS RULES OUT APPEAL AGAINST COMPENSATION REFUSAL"

"Sion Jenkins today said he would not appeal against a decision to refuse him compensation for the six years he spent in prison, before being cleared of murdering his foster-daughter Billie-Jo. Jenkins, who was convicted in 1998 of murdering the 13-year-old, has written in a book about the case, in which he claims to have uncovered information about a possible suspect. His conviction was declared unsafe on appeal in 2004. Two subsequent trials ended with jurors failing to reach a verdict, and the former teacher was eventually cleared in 2006. Details of the Ministry of Justice's rejection of the reported £500,000 claim for his time in prison, emerged this week. In an interview with the Press Association, Jenkins said he had not given the refusal 'a second thought'.

"I am not appealing the decision because it's not important", he added.

"The most important thing for me is that the investigation doesn't die, and that Sussex Police continue to look for leads."

He said he believed receiving compensation would not have convinced people he was innocent of murdering his foster-daughter, 'because of their own prejudices'. Despite playing down the rejection, he described it as 'bizarre' that people could be locked up for years and then not receive any compensation. Referring to the Ministry of Justice statement which said the appeal court had made it clear compensation should be paid when someone had been shown to be 'clearly innocent', Jenkins said the Ministry had

"effectively put another demand on any miscarriage, to prove innocence as opposed to the traditional burden on the prosecution of proving guilt".

In his book, *The Murder of Billie-Jo,* he said he had

identified a possible new suspect. Jenkins said he spoke to someone he thought was a dark-haired, plain-clothed police officer in his hallway in the confused hour after Billie-Jo was found dead.

"I don't know who that person was, so that"s another lead and there are other leads that I think should be looked at", Jenkins said.

"I don't want avenues closed down. It's hard enough trying to solve a crime 13 or 14 years after the event, without closing down particular leads."

Sussex Police have said that the Billie-Jo murder case remains 'unsolved' but they continue to actively pursue any new leads of inquiry that emerge".

Source: The Guardian Online, 11 August 2010. Author: Haroon Siddique and Agencies.

"SION JENKINS: THE HOME OFFICE DECIDES THAT 'NOT GUILTY' IS DIFFERENT FROM 'INNOCENT'"

"Innocence, it was decreed by the Home Office last week, is much more than just not being convicted of a crime, much to the surprise of some people, who believe that a compensation 'culture' is ingrained in our society. It was revealed that the Ministry of Justice had ruled that no money was to be paid to a man who had spent six years in jail for a murder he was later cleared of committing because he had not been shown to be *"clearly innocent"*. The case of the former schoolteacher Sion Jenkins had rewritten legal textbooks even before it illustrated the controversial use of compensating those wrongly convicted of crimes.

Jenkins' claim for a reported £500,000 was refused by the government last week. Jenkins, 52, was jailed in 1998 for the murder of his foster-daughter Billie-Jo in 1997. The conviction was quashed on appeal and two retrials ended with juries unable to reach a decision. It was clear the legal avenues had been pretty much exhausted and no further retrial was ordered. Jenkins was found not guilty and released. Officials said that the Court of Appeal had clear guidelines concerning when compensation should be paid. New evidence must 'prove innocence' rather than a prosecution simply being too weak. Campaigners say that the interpretation of the guidelines are not only unfair, but undermine decisions of judges and juries.

Jenkins' supporters attacked the Ministry of Justice's decision as 'insidious' and added "in which universe does not guilty mean not innocent?"

The decision was seen by some as a snub to the jury system, and a further injustice in the compensation procedure for victims of miscarriages of justice. In some cases, those who are awarded compensation have money deducted for 'board and lodging', the costs of living in a prison cell. Harry Fletcher, of the National Association of Probation Officers said: "It seems to me that the absolute minimum is paid to people, and so many deductions as possible are made, quite apart from the time people have to wait. When someone is cleared of a crime, they just walk out through the court doors, they don't qualify for probation support or assistance. It's not just the finances, there's the assessment of their needs, and it's extraordinary difficult for people to adapt. The Home Office clearly thinks that Jenkins was freed on a 'technicality', which doesn't mean he's 'innocent', but that's not for them to decide. It's fairly shameful for them to think they can overrule the court".

Source: The Guardian Online, 15 August 2010. Author: Tracy McVeigh.

"WHO WAS BILLIE-JO JENKINS AS DETECTIVES REVEAL HOPE OF FRESH DNA COULD SOLVE SCHOOLGIRL'S 1997 MURDER"

"Cold-case detectives with Sussex Police hope fresh DNA and blood tests could finally solve the murder of Sussex schoolgirl Billie-Jo Jenkins. The teenager was beaten to death with an iron tent peg at her home in Hastings, East Sussex, 25 years ago this month. Sussex Police renewed their appeal for information in what has become one of the UK's most high-profile unsolved murders. Billie-Jo had been painting patio doors at her home next to Alexandra Park. Her foster-father, Sion Jenkins, who was a deputy headteacher at the time, was convicted of her murder but was formally acquitted in 2006 after a second re-trial.

The key disputed evidence involved microscopic drops of Billie-Jo's blood on Mr Jenkins' clothing. Sion Jenkins lost his bid for compensation for the six years he spent in prison. Last year, the website *Justice for Sion Jenkins* said:

"The story of Billie-Jo can't have a happy ending, but it should have a truthful one. Someone knows the answer, and it's time to tell the truth".

It called on Sussex Police to re-open the case and "admit that serious mistakes were made in 1997". Sussex Police will now re-examine crime scene exhibits to see if advances in forensic science can deliver a breakthrough in the case.

Officials have said the review is part of a regular assessment process where each unsolved homicide is assessed two-yearly to examine any new information that may have become available which would mean they could re-open the investigation. In a statement, the force said: "Currently, no new information has been provided in this case, and it is not being re-investigated. However, as part of the regular assessment process, we are currently carrying out a forensic review of material held on the case in order to establish whether or not scientific advances can provide new evidence or lines of enquiry. We will always examine any new information on forensic opportunities which might lead to new lines of enquiry whenever they arise. Anyone who has any new information on the case is being asked to contact the force on 101, quoting 'Operation Cathedral'".

Source: ITV News Online, 1 February 2022 (www.ITV.com / news/ meridian.

CHAPTER SEVEN

THE CASE IN RETROSPECT

TIME- LINE OF THE CASE

<u>1997</u>

15 February: Billie-Jo Jenkins murdered.

16: Annie and Charlotte Jenkins First Police Interviews.

17: First Suspect, Mark Lynam, arrested.

18: Sion and Lois attend press conference. Mark Lynam detained under Mental Health Act, detained in secure psychiatric unit.

19: Lois and friend, Peter Gaimster, inform police of suspicions regarding Felix Simmons, who is arrested as second suspect.

20: Simmons released.

24: Sion Jenkins, third suspect arrested.

25: Sussex Police inform Lois Jenkins and Denise Lancaster that Sion murdered Billie-Jo. Annie's second police interview. Sion Jenkins released.

26: Sion leaves Hastings to stay with parents in Aberystwyth.

13 March: Sion re-arrested.

14: Sion charged with murder, held on remand.

20: Sussex police debrief the children informing them that their father murdered Billie-Jo.

26: Sion granted bail, returns to parents in Wales.

1998
3 June: First trial begins.
2 July: Sion convicted and sentenced to life imprisonment.
21 December: Leave to appeal granted.

1999
30 November: First appeal begins.
21 December: First appeal Dismissed.

2000
14 January: Appeal to the House of Lords refused.

2002
5 February: Annie and Charlotte re-interviewed.

2003
12 May: Case referred back to appeal by CCRC.
23 July: Lois Jenkins makes third statement to police denying daughters' evidence.

2004
30 June: Sion Jenkins' second appeal begins.
16 July: Appeal successful. Conviction quashed. Re-trial ordered.
2 August: Sion granted bail and leaves prison.

2005
7 February: Sion marries Tina Ferneyhough.
28 April: Second trial begins.
11 July: Trial ends, jury unable to agree.
31 October: Third trial begins.

2006
9 February: Jury still unable to agree a verdict. Sion Jenkins is acquitted.

Source: The Murder of Billie-Jo – Sion Jenkins and Bob Woffinden: Chronology- pp ix-xi.

THE CASE FOR THE PROSECUTION

The prosecution contended that Sion Jenkins murdered his foster-daughter in the time period between arriving home from collecting Charlotte from her clarinet lesson and leaving to go to the DIY store. His daughters, Annie and Charlotte, were waiting outside at the front of the house when he committed the act. He had approximately three minutes alone in order to commit the crime.

Jenkins' initial statement to the police was that he did not go into the house at all, but waited outside with Annie while Charlotte dropped off her clarinet. However, in a later statement he admitted that he had gone into the house, but did not see Billie-Jo. It was speculated by the police that he initially lied about not going into the house to distance himself from the crime scene. However, he later changed his account because his statements differed from both his daughters, Charlotte and Annie.

Jenkins said in his first 999 call to the ambulance service, that he had been away from the home for between 30 and 45 minutes. However, the reconstructed timed police drive to and from the DIY store took approximately 15 minutes. In his statements to the police, Jenkins said that he simply drove to the store and back home without going into the store or even getting out of the car. How then could he claim that this short car journey could have taken over half an hour? This does suggest that he was lying to give himself the longest possible alibi.

In addition, the journey to the DIY store itself appears strange, particularly since there was an adequate supply of white spirits already in the house. Police suspected that it had been entirely manufactured as a reason for Jenkins to distance himself from the crime and create an alibi.

In his second 999 call to the ambulance service, Jenkins told the operator that he had turned Billie-Jo over and placed her in the recovery position. This was untrue because he did not do this, and he even later admitted this.

In addition to this specific lie, paramedics attending the scene observed that Jenkins had done nothing to try and help Billie-Jo. Given that he later claimed that the blood on his clothes was due to Billie-Jo exhaling onto him, then he must have believed that she was still alive, which in itself, appears suspect. Police were also curious why, when he saw Billie-Jo's battered body, he spent valuable time calming his other two daughters rather than calling an ambulance immediately, particularly if he really believed Billie-Jo was still alive.

His other observed odd behaviour raised suspicions. Ambulance staff found it odd that Jenkins did not stay with Billie-Jo as they were attending to her. Instead, he went to the front of the house and just sat in his MG car. Police suspected this was to provide an excuse for any of Billie-Jo's blood being found in his car, in case he transferred it on his journey to the DIY store.

Further police inquiries revealed that Jenkins had lied on his CV when he applied for the post of deputy headteacher in Hastings. He further lied about the school he attended as a youth, about the university he attended, the degree he obtained and other academic qualifications he was supposed to possess.

As a motive for the killing, the prosecution suggested that the day of the murder had been a frustrating one for Jenkins. There had been a series of petty mishaps involving wasted journeys. According to his wife, Lois, Jenkins had argued with Billie-Jo earlier in the day. Did something Billie-Jo say or do trigger an outburst so violent that he beat her around the head?

There is no evidence of an intruder and no known motive for anyone to kill Billie-Jo. She had defence wounds from blows to her arms, but there were no signs of any prior struggle or nothing to suggest that she attempted to escape from her attacker. There was no evidence to suggest a sexual assault had been attempted on Billie-Jo. Whoever carried out the vicious attack went straight to bludgeoning her in the head. They didn't even need to bring a weapon with them as they used one previously placed in the patio by daughter, Annie, after clearing out the utility room. Sion Jenkins was the only one person who knew it was there.

Police asked Sion and Lois Jenkins to make a public appeal following the murder. Shortly after this, Sion came under suspicion and then became the chief suspect in the crime. He had been the last person to see Billie-Jo alive, and the first adult to discover her body.

THE CASE FOR THE DEFENCE

How could someone commit this crime within three minutes as the prosecution alleged? A few minutes was the absolute maximum amount of time anyone's statements have allowed that Sion Jenkins was alone with Billie-Jo, between the journey to collect Charlotte from her clarinet lesson, return home, and then going on the journey to the DIY store.

Annie's second police statements confirm how brief the time really was. This is an incredibly short amount of time for someone's anger to be triggered, to bludgeon someone to death, to stuff part of a bin liner into a nostril, clean up, and finally compose themselves. Neither of Sion's two daughters reported noticing any blood on Sion's clothing at that point.

Sion Jenkins testified that when he found his foster-daughter's body, there was a small bubble on her nose which later disappeared. His defence argued that blood patterns found on his clothing could have been caused by this blood bubble bursting when Sion was close up to her.

The consultant neurosurgeon called for the defence at the first trial said that in his opinion, and based on the amount of blood present at the scene, Billie-Jo could have been breathing for between 15 and 20 minutes following the attack on her.

The pivotal evidence in Sion Jenkins' successful appeal in 2004, and in the subsequent re-trials, came from Professor David Denison, one of the UK's leading experts on lung disease. He found evidence of what he believed was a rare medical condition called Pulmonary Interstitial Emphysema or PIE. This resulted in a build-up of pressure in Billie-Jo's lungs which occurred in the minutes after the attack and before she died. He believed this was caused by blood blocking her airways, and that some of this blood was released as a result of Sion Jenkins moving her.

This resulted in a spray of droplets landing on Sion's clothing, known medically as expiration spatter. Professor Denison reconstructed the conditions of the murder, this time taking into account the pressure in Billie-Jo's lungs, and created a 'similar pattern of blood staining'.

He explained:

"My experiments show that you can create from the mouth and nose, the sort of spatter that were present on Sion Jenkins' clothing, and the distribution is 'almost identical' and the size of the droplets is also almost identical, so it is a very credible explanation".

Both the prosecution and the defence presented compelling blood spatter evidence at the two re-trials. However, the bone fragment evidence was never admitted. This does beg a question: would this have really been a game changer? How much weight should be placed on the journey to the DIY store, Sion Jenkins' changing statements and his unusual behaviour at the time? Do all these taken together, confirm guilt beyond reasonable doubt?

SUMMARY OF THE FORENSIC EVIDENCE IN THE CASE

The critical evidence in the Jenkins' case was essentially scientific. Microscopic examination of Sion Jenkins' clothing revealed 158 bloodspots which were distributed on his right leg, left leg, fleece jacket and left shoe. However, significantly, there were no cast-off drops found anywhere on his clothing.

DNA analysis confirmed that all the blood on Jenkins' clothing was Billie-Jo's. There was no blood found on the clothing of his neighbour, Denise Lancaster, or on either of the two paramedics attending Billie-Jo. However, there was no broad area of bloodstaining on Jenkins' clothing which would have been present if he had cradled Billie-Jo in his arms.

Forensic tests revealed that Billie-Jo had been bludgeoned at very close range and that the blows inflicted on her were considerable. Consequently, it was suggested that the assailant must have been in very close contact with the victim at the time of the attack.

On discovering Billie-Jo, Sion Jenkins had, at some stage, leant over Billie-Jo and noticed what he later described as a "bubble of blood" at her nose. According to Billie-Jo's post-mortem report, blood was found in her airways. In addition, her lungs were found to be hyper-inflated, which means they were fully extended with air trapped within them.

Jenkins' defence team believed that at some point following the attack, Billie-Jo had exhaled a fine bloody mist over Sion as he leant over to attend to her. This raised the key question: was the blood found on Jenkins' clothing caused by impact spatter as suggested by the prosecution, or by exhalation spray as contended by the defence?

The amount of blood present at the murder scene indicated that Billie-Jo's heart must have been pumping blood around her body. This is indicative of the vital fact that she must have still been alive after the attack.

Forensic experts for the defence stated that the pattern of staining to that produced on Sion Jenkins' clothing could only have been produced by exhalation and not by impact spatter. To counter this theory, the prosecution maintained that it would have been necessary for Billie-Jo to have inhaled a significant amount of air for her to have expirated the blood droplets found on Jenkins' clothing. This involved vigorous breathing movements which would have been impossible, given her dying state.

However, in order for the prosecution's theory (that Sion Jenkins killed Billie-Jo) to be sustained, they had to demonstrate conclusively that it was virtually impossible for Billie-Jo to have still been alive when Sion Jenkins discovered her. Therefore, it would have been impossible for her to have expirated the blood found on Jenkins' clothing.

Consequently, the only possible explanation for the presence of these bloodspots was that it had been caused by impact spatter and not the result of expiration However, to counter this suggestion, defence expert Professor David Denison reported that if Billie-Jo's airways contained blood and she had breathed out, this would result in the kind of spray seen on Sion Jenkins' clothing.

He further argued that a single exhalation could produce all the bloodspots found on Sion's clothing. He also maintained that this exhalation could have been passive, inaudible and invisible, and even occurring after death. Professor Denison also pointed out that there must have been a blockage in Billie-Jo's upper airways. When this blockage was eased, the build-up of air trapped in her lungs would have been released under pressure. It was this that caused the exhalation spray.

Examination of slides of sections of Billie-Jo's lungs, led to the discovery that Billie-Jo had Pulmonary Interstitial

Emphysema or PIE. This occurs when a person is making violent attempts to breathe but the main airways have become blocked.

This presence of PIE proved two important factors, firstly that Billie-Jo did not die instantly because time had elapsed to enable the changes to have taken place, and secondly, that she had a blockage of the airway.

The prosecution commissioned further analysis of the scientific evidence. An examination of the surviving bloodspots detected white spots within the bloodspots themselves.

According to the prosecution, these white spots could have come from damaged tissue on Billie-Jo's scalp. The prosecution's strategy at the first re-trial in 2005, was two-fold; to reject the defence's theory of PIE and the expirated spray, and to construct its own case comprising of the new discovery of the presence of what became known as the 'white inclusions'.

The prosecution maintained that these new inclusions would prove that Sion Jenkins had violently attacked Billie-Jo, on the basis that particles of skin in addition the blood had landed on Jenkins' clothing. Following the prosecution's disclosure of these new inclusions, Jenkins' defence team consulted leading experts to assess the scientific aspects of the prosecution's revised case.

Three of the world's authorities in the field of PIE, concluded that the evidence of PIE in the tissue slides of Billie-Jo's lung tissue was "absolutely unequivocal". Consequently, they found the 'white inclusions' argument to be 'specious'.

The 158 bloodspots found on Sion Jenkins' clothing in effect, amounted to one drop of blood roughly 1/20th of a millilitre. To place these microscopic bloodspots in proportion, a vigorous sneeze will normally generate around 20,000 tiny droplets of mucus, saliva and phlegm. This is roughly about 100 times as many as the number found on Sion Jenkins' clothing. What must not be overlooked is that Billie-Jo's airways would certainly have been damaged by the forceable insertion of the plastic bin-liner into her left nostril. As the result, her ethmoid bone had been fractured. Therefore, it would not be surprising that microscopic fragments of skin, bone and even brain, would all be present in the expirated blood.

Defence experts carried out experiments in ambient air currents to establish how blood droplets would travel in the atmosphere and environmental conditions expected on the Jenkins' patio in Hastings. They concluded that droplets expelled by Billie-Jo would have landed on Sion Jenkins' clothing.

The evidence was also examined by a forensic consultant specialising in the field of bloodstain spatter evidence. His conclusions were that the pattern of bloodstaining on Sion Jenkins' fleece jacket was

"consistent only with the blood being expirated from a 'blood contaminated' airway. In order for the patterns seen on the clothing to be recreated, Sion Jenkins would have to be in a 'crouching' semi-kneeling position, with the right leg and right, lower leg exposed to the blood source, and his torso twisted right and lowered to expose the inner chest area. This was a position inconsistent with him having been the assailant, but consistent with him positioning himself to examine Billie-Jo".

He also added that the prosecution's theory, that the pattern had been created by impact spatter was highly improbable.

At Sion Jenkins' first re-trial in 2005, defence counsel, Christopher Sallen, QC, submitted to the jury that the scenes-of-crime work carried out at the Jenkins' home, had not been particularly thorough. Many bloodspots over the patio area had not been taken into consideration by the prosecution. For example, there were two trellises outside, and one had been removed but the wall behind had not been examined. Significantly, many spots at some greater distance from Billie-Jo's body had also not been examined.

The location and size of these spots did indicate a dynamic attack had taken place This strongly suggested that there was a high probability that the assailant would have intercepted a lot of blood spatter. There was no evidence of this on Sion Jenkins' clothing.

There was another vital piece of evidence which appears to have been overlooked: a clearly visible footprint on the patio surface. Billie-Jo had swept the patio that afternoon before commencing her painting of the doors. The footprint could therefore not have been there earlier. It appeared to be the print of a male wearing boots with patterned soles. This footprint did not match Sion Jenkins, nor any other member of the Jenkins' family. Also, it did not match any member of the emergency services who attended the crime scene.

The only logical conclusion to be drawn from this evidence is that the print must have belonged to the assailant. In fact, one of the attending paramedics noticed this muddy footprint on Billie-Jo's leggings. However, when Billie-Jo's body was removed from the scene, these prints were lost. This was persuasive evidence to the effect that both the killer's footwear was likely to leave impressions, a fact obviously overlooked. Also, by standing on the body of Billie-Jo, the assailant was displaying what can only be described as uncontrollable and deranged behaviour.

Billie-Jo had defended herself against her attacker because defence wounds were found on her body. The position of these wounds strongly suggests that the assailant had been in different positions when attacking her, and could very likely have shed blood himself. Regrettably, this crucial evidence was lost due to inadequate crime-scene examination and preservation. What the prosecution had purported to have discovered in their new evidence was that bloodspots on Sion Jenkins' clothing not just Billie-Jo's blood, but also portions of skin, tissue, bone, specks of paint and fragments of metal had been discovered. The obvious insinuation here was that the prosecution was seeking to establish that minute traces of the murder weapon itself, the tent-peg, had now been found on Sion Jenkins' clothing. This, the prosecution regarded as 'dramatic new evidence'.

The prosecution in Sion Jenkins' original trial in 1998, had argued on the basis that the microscopic bloodspots were evidence that proved Sion Jenkins was guilty of the murder. By the first re-trial in 2005, the prosecution had been continued on the basis that it was the 'white inclusions' that now provided the scientific underpinning of the prosecution case.

By the second re-trial later in 2005, the prosecution was brought on the basis that guilt could be proved not by the invisible bloodspots themselves, nor by the 'white inclusions', but by even more microscopic fragments found within the 'white inclusions' that lay within the invisible spots.

In fact, it turned out that fragments of human material, whether bone, brain matter or anything else, were not present within these fragments. As for the minute fragments of metal, there was no connection between this piece of metal and the murder weapon. It was confirmed that it was not from the tent peg.

John Sinar, the consultant neurosurgeon at Middlesborough General Hospital, in his Second Report for the defence, emphasised a number of highly relevant points. One in particular was:

"Sion had no brain matter on his clothing, when this would certainly have been anticipated had he been the assailant, since brain matter was clearly seen in Billie-Jo's hair, and that contused brain could well have been

transferred to the assailant".

SION JENKINS' REFLECTIONS ON THE CASE - A SELECTION

"The Crown had originally maintained that my note-taking was indicative of a guilty man trying to get his story straight. However, DC Hutt had not given evidence at the first trial. Once they did call him to give evidence at the second trial, he acknowledged that he had recommended the note-taking course of action. This point, the prosecution had to drop at the third trial." (1)

"As soon as I heard Nicholas Hilliard's new opening speech, I knew that the trial was going to be presented differently. The emphasis was going to be less on fact and more on innuendo. The Crown was distancing itself from the forensic science and medical evidence, and relying more on presenting me as a bad and devious character who almost regardless of evidence, deserved to be convicted

So long-forgotten family incidents were now being aired out of context, and blown out of all proportion. One of the age-old sayings, we all learn as we grow up, 'that it's the exception that proves the rule'. Yet, with both the law and the media today, uncharacteristic incidents are reported as if they are characteristic, the very opposite of what they actually are. In that way, the exception becomes the rule, and what has been common sense for hundreds of years, is turned on its head." (2).

"Throughout the history of my case, there was persistent anxiety about the way in which it was being reported, but *The Times* was the only newspaper ever singled out for a judicial reprimand." (3)

"Chris Sallon (defence counsel) concluded his cross-examination of Lois by explaining to the jury that the defence had discovered that she had taken on a literary agent who specialised in non-fiction accounts of true crime. When this was put to her, she said she no longer had any intentions of writing a book, but didn't deny that the agent was acting for her. So, she had a financial interest in the outcome of the trial. She'd make money in any event, but it stood to reason she'd make more if I were convicted." (4)

"Some readers may point out that I was bound to do better a second time (the third trial) having already had a full rehearsal. I would agree, but I'd point out that such a factor applies to all re-trials. Since many witnesses, whether prosecution or defence, will have done it all before, then the repeated process becomes even more artificial than it was the first time. Those responsible for the Criminal Justice System should not be encouraging re-trials, but working out how to avoid them." (5)

"<u>The Final Trial</u> In his closing speech, Nicholas Hilliard (prosecution) told the jury that they could set the scientific evidence to one side and still comfortably convict me. By the end, the Crown was trying hard to disassociate itself from the claims it had once put forward as established fact; that the scientific evidence itself proved that I had killed Billie-Jo, and to obtain a conviction on the basis of character assassination. Obviously, I thought it an immoral prosecution from the outset but as it had gone on, it really had become a lowest common denominator case. The Crown had ditched the evidence; all they had left was prejudice. I was an unsavoury character, and therefore, although there was no evidence, I must have done it." (6)

"Not only were the reports uninformed, but they made damned sure they stayed uninformed. Newsrooms had prejudged the outcome of the case; they were going to write what they were going to write. The inviolable tradition of gutter journalism 'never let the facts get in the way of a good story' would prevail. What this outburst of media hostility betrayed was a collective abrogation of journalistic responsibilities." (7)

"One suspects that the default approach of newspapers is one of pure malice; after all, it makes 'better' copy. In this respect, the most dispiriting aspect of gutter journalism in Britain today, is that it is no longer confined to the 'gutter press'. It appears to have defied gravity to seep out of the gutter and into more elevated sections of the media. The headlines produced at the end of the third trial revealed that the media had constructed its own image of Sion. When he woke up on Saturday morning, 15 February, 1997, he was a deputy headteacher with no criminal record, and against whom there wasn't a shred of suspicion of misconduct. By the time of the acquittal, the media had turned the family man into an unsavoury and deeply dislikeable bully. It was a picture that had no basis in reality, and existed only in the media's imagination. Nevertheless, it was one that seeped into the public's collective consciousness." (8)

"Judges are often accused of not living in the real world. Though the criticism is generally misplaced, this is one of those rare occasions where it would be amply justified." (9)

EPILOGUE

"Life is often unpredictable and uncertain, yet when reviewing the efficacy of the Criminal Justice System, we prefer to think in terms of certainties, that the guilty are convicted and that the innocent are acquitted. We accept that mistakes might occasionally be made, that we have the Court of Appeal to correct any failures in justice. But those who have been there, who have experienced wrongful conviction, they know that success following this route is fraught with difficulties. When someone is convicted of a serious offence, despite being innocent, it is nothing short of a miracle if they persuade the Court of Appeal that their conviction is unsafe. For many who have experienced the Court of Appeal, the Court appears to be no more than a body whose function is simple to uphold and rubber-stamp the decision of the first tribunal. Some would argue that justice, in this context, is more about protecting the system and those individuals who work within it, rather than correcting injustice. The unpalatable truth is that too many men and women, through no fault of their own, are serving long sentences for crimes they did not commit. They have been failed by a system they probably once believed in. It is this system we all share as fellow citizens." (10)

Source: "The Murder of Billie-Jo" by Sion Jenkins and Bob Woffinden

(1) Page 349 (6) Page 360

(2) Page 350 (7) Page 371

(3) Page 353 (8) Page 375

(4) Page 354 (9) Page 405

(5) Page 358 (10) Page 435

This work concludes by including an informative article which centres on issues not previously highlighted in discussions on this particular case. This article provides highly relevant questions which the reader should consider in reaching their own conclusions about this tragic yet thought-provoking case.

IMPORTANT QUESTIONS

1. How did the police handle the case?

"Hastings police were desperate to make an arrest in the town, which had become the focus of negative publicity in the national press. Several murders in Hastings remained unsolved, and public confidence in the police was at a very low ebb. The police made lots of reassuring statements, but they seemed to be getting nowhere. Although they were given many leads by concerned members of the public, they failed to follow up plausible lines of enquiry. By the time a month had passed, they were under real pressure for several reasons, not least of which was their public image.

2 .Why were the issues confused?

When the police announced that they had charged Sion Jenkins with the murder of his foster-daughter, they made an explicit link with the deception charge over his qualifications. Early evening TV news headlines on 14 March 1997 led with the joint allegation. Widespread coverage followed in the national newspapers. Sion Jenkins was established in the public perception as 'the teacher who had lied'.

The implied connection was that if he had lied about his qualifications, then his denial of murder was bound to be a lie. The connection is illogical. Police did not follow up the deception charge but they used it from the outset to slant the case against Sion Jenkins. By the time the case came to trial fifteen months later, the idea of guilt by association was established.

3. A Fair Trial?

The trial was held at Lewes Crown Court in East

Sussex. As the county town, Lewes is the location of the Education Department which had employed Sion Jenkins, as well as the Crown Court where he was tried. Gossip and rumour had circulated relentlessly in the county during the time since he was charged.

Individuals connected in various ways with the legal system had not hesitated to voice personal opinions in an unprofessional way. In these circumstances, was it really possible for Sion Jenkins to have a fair trial in East Sussex?

4. A Credible Motive?

There was none. The prosecution at the original trial was emphatic on this point. The re-trial offered no more clarity. At the retrial one motive suggested was that Sion Jenkins was under stress because he was worried about having lied on his CV. Quite how this might have caused him to murder Billie-Jo was never explained. It was public knowledge that he was to become the next headteacher.

An even less-likely motive was plucked from Peter Gaimster's unfounded allegation that Sion Jenkins had kicked Billie-Jo the previous summer, a fact which evidently Gaimster "had kept to himself until several months after the murder". Nicholas Hilliard seemed to suggest that the motive for murder was to prevent Billie-Jo revealing that he had been violent the previous year. That was as good as it got.

5. Realistic Opportunity?

The evidence showed that there would not have been time for Sion Jenkins (who was actually with two of his other daughters) to commit the brutal murder and conceal what had taken place.

6. Compelling Evidence?

At the time of the murder, the police asserted that there would have been a great deal of direct evidence to link the murderer to the scene. However, by the time of the trial and after months of strenuous efforts to link Sion Jenkins with the crime, the prosecution could offer only the most tenuous circumstantial and ambiguous forensic evidence, based on invisible spots of blood.

7. An Orchestrated Smear Campaign?

On 2 July 1998, moments after the verdict was announced on television, Lois Jenkins' solicitor was reading out a denunciation of Sion Jenkins. It appeared in all the newspapers the following morning. The initial timing and content of the statement suggested that it was not a spontaneous reaction to the verdict.

The campaign had begun and continued throughout the following week and beyond. How was it possible for reporters to show copies of Sion Jenkins' CV on television? That charge had not been pursued. The document would have still constituted evidence in any proceedings on the deception charge and in any event, application forms remain confidential documents.

Police sources were frequently quoted, for example, the *Daily Mail* of 3 July 1998 quoted police officers as saying that Lois Jenkins had always feared her husband would injure her and that Billie-Jo had been wearing some of Lois's old clothing on the day of the murder. Note that this apparent evidence was given after the verdict, when Sion Jenkins was already in prison.

In August 1998, the *News of the World* published the completely untrue story that Sion Jenkins had made a cell confession a month after being convicted. Top police officers made comments. Detective Superintendent Jeremy

Paine was quoted as saying the police "remain interested in any relevant evidence relating to the Jenkins' case". Why, if they had done their job properly? With the accused serving a life sentence, what further evidence could be relevant? This was a classic case of nailing down the coffin lid.

8. A Police PR Opportunity?

By the time Sion Jenkins' trial began on 3 June 1998, Sussex Police were having difficulties with their public image. In January 1998, there had been the fatal shooting of the unarmed and naked James Ashley in St. Leonards, resulting in the suspension of police officers. In consecutive weeks in that same month, January 1998, two women were murdered in Hastings. No one has yet been charged with those murders.

In February 1998, the conviction of Sheila Bowler for murder was overturned at a retrial. This case is described in the book *Anybody's Nightmare – the Sheila Bowler Story*. This account revealed strange similarities between the Sheila Bowler case and that of Sion Jenkins.

On 8 June 1998, as the Jenkins' trial was getting underway, the case of two women accused of the murder of Richard Watson in East Grinstead collapsed. Investigative journalist, Bob Woffinden, who examined the James Hanratty case, wrote a detailed analysis of the Watson case in *The Guardian* (10 April, 1999). The parallels with the Sion Jenkins case were unmistakable.

In August 1998, PATROL, the Sussex police news sheet, explicitly linked the Watson case with the Jenkins case, stressing that "both were investigated with the same high degree of integrity and professionalism". It claimed that media coverage after the East Sussex trial had "reflected most favourably on the skill and sensitivity of the police inquiry".

The outcome of the Jenkins case provided a convenient and much-needed boost to the reputation of the force. In December 1998, five officers received commendations for their work on the case. One of the commendations referred to the work involving going "far beyond that which could be expected of an officer".

Could it be that their recent bad publicity explained the determination of the police to show that this time they really had got their man?

9. What was the Role of Social Services?

This tragic case involved the death of a child in care. Her death, it is now claimed, was at the hands of someone into whose care Social Services had placed her. Did the system really fail Billie-Jo Jenkins? If Sion Jenkins were guilty, the social workers involved failed over five years to recognise the risks presented by this placement. What did the records over these five years show? What about their routine reviews? What did the inquiry reveal?

Lois Jenkins, herself a social worker, failed to alert Social Services to what she claimed (after the verdict) had been years of her husband's brutality. If this was the case, how could she, with her professional knowledge and background, have introduced a vulnerable child into an abusive household?

In *The Times* of 3 July 1998, Billie-Jo's aunt Margaret Coster, was quoted as saying that Lois told her she would not leave Billie-Jo alone with Sion. If this was indeed the truth, how could either of these women have allowed Billie-Jo to continue being at risk? A family friend claims to have witnessed Billie-Jo being viciously kicked during a holiday in France the previous summer. Would responsible adults just stand by?

Such allegations are hard to reconcile with the fact that Lois Jenkins went ahead with taking on the joint legal guardianship of Billie-Jo very shortly before the murder. Or did Social Services, in fact, carry out their job responsibly?

Billie-Jo, from all accounts prior to the verdict, had become a confident, lively teenager, coping increasingly successfully with life as a much-loved child in her foster family. Unless all these accounts are untrue, Social Services correctly discharged their responsibilities to all concerned.

At the time of the case, the distorted media presentation of the family's life served only to obscure the weakness of the evidence leading to the conviction of Sion Jenkins.

There are two possibilities. Either Social Services failed abysmally to protect a child at risk, a failure which merits considerable public scrutiny and demands accountability, or Social Services were unfairly implicated in a misrepresentation of the truth in order to convict Sion Jenkins.

10. Trial by Media?

Before, during and after the trial, there was sensational media coverage which demonised Sion Jenkins and presented a tragedy in the terms of a soap opera. Even the broadsheets could not resist stereotypes which oversimplified the situation and caricatured the individuals involved.

The media have undeniably played their part in distorting the facts of this case. This campaign challenged them over the years to investigate just who had been lying about what, to show they had the will to reveal the truth, and in doing so, to help to expose a very real injustice.

Astonishingly, during such an important and high-profile retrial, reporting of events was spasmodic. Even after the outcome, the focus was not on the evidence, but on rumour and allegations about his character. Sion Jenkins has been cleared of all charges, but there is still a burning need to know how such a terrible miscarriage of justice was allowed to happen, and to expose those responsible. We invite the media to probe, to ask awkward questions, and to pursue the truth until people have the facts they need to know because this is, truly, in the public interest, and for the public good."

Source: justiceforsionjenkins.org.uk / Important Questions.

REFERENCES AND BIBLIOGRAPHY

PUBLICATIONS

Craig, A, *"Bloodstain Pattern Analysis: Forensic Evidence in Court: Evaluation and Scientific Opinion"* (John Wiley and Son, Chichester, 2016).

Gibson, C, *"Case turned on 158 spots of blood"* (BBC News Online, 9 February 2006).

Gray, S, *"Profile: The Contradictions of Sion Jenkins"* (Times Online, 9 February 2006).

James, A *"Court of Appeal: Fresh Evidence, Ordering of Retrial"* (Journal of Criminal Law, 1, February 2005, **69**, (1) 16).

Jenkins, S & Woffinden, B, *"The Murder of Billie-Jo"* (John Blake Publishing Ltd, London, 2008).

Woffinden, B. *"Wrong Again: Sion Jenkins is Innocent"* (New Statesman, 11 July 1998).

OFFICIAL REPORTS

<u>Appeal 1999</u>: R v Jenkins (Sion David Charles). Case No 98/4720/WB - Transcript: Royal Courts of Justice, 21 December 1999.

<u>Appeal 2004</u>: R v Sion David Charles Jenkins. Case No 2003/02883/B4. Transcript: Royal Courts of Justice, 16, July, 2004.

"Statement of Reasons: Criminal Cases Review Commission: Second Appeal. Ref: 00226/2001/Jenkins.

RESEARCH PAPER

"Miscarriages of Justice: The Uncertainty Principle" Dennis Eady, Ph.D. Thesis: School of Social Science, Cardiff University, July 2009 - Chapter 14.

MEDIA SOURCES

BBC Online News.
The Independent.
The Guardian.
The Daily Mail.
British Library (Newspaper Archives).
Hastings and St. Leonards Observer.
Timesonline.co.uk
The Free Library.co.uk
www.justiceforsionjenkins.org.uk

TV Documentary: *"Tonight with Trevor McDonald"*- ITV, 20, March, 2006.

Words Are Life's Best Selling Title

Sold world-wide to libraries, educational establishments and individuals, this is *"The Pendle Witch Trials of 1612"*.

What it doesn't do...

Sensationalise the historic trials and associated events.

Fictionalise the already-fascinating characters involved.

Romanticise or demonise the women accused of witchcraft— or their families.

What it does...

It provides an accurate account and overview of the court proceedings of 1612, and leaves the reader to make their own decision regarding the truth behind the infamous trials.

Currently available on Amazon

Kindle £3.50 and Paperback £5.50

ISBN: 9781797806679

www.wordarelife.co.uk

wordsarelife@mail.com